TOTAL
BABY
knits

Produced for Leisure Arts by MQ Publications Limited
MQ Publications New York office:
49 West 24th Street, 8th floor
New York, NY 10010
Phone: (+1) 212 223 6342
London office:
12 The Ivories
6–8 Northampton Street
London N1 2HY
Phone: + 44 (0)20 7359 2244
Website: www.mqpublications.com

Publisher and CEO: Zaro Weil
Group Sales Director: Simon Majumdar
Vice President of Sales and Marketing, North America: Stacey Ashton
Editorial Director: Ljiljana Baird
Editor: Sorrel Wood
Developmental Editor: BJ Berti
Technical Editor: Mari Lynn Patrick
Fashion Photography: Jennifer Lèvy
Steps Photography: Lizzie Orme
Design: Joanna Hill, Redbox Design

Made in the United States of America. Third Printing.

International Standard Book Number 1-57486-581-1

TOTAL BABY *knits*

CANDI JENSEN

contents

THE PROJECTS

introduction

Designing knitwear has always been a pleasure for me, but designing for babies and toddlers holds a special place in my heart. From the time I picked up the needles to make a sweater for my new baby girl many years ago, I knew I would be creating something special—a sweater that might not be perfect, but would certainly reflect my overwhelming joy, and was sure to be cherished for years to come.

Now, when I'm sitting down to design for the new babies out there, I think about how charming and perfect they will look in each garment. How cute they will look in a cheerful sweater or a brightly colored hat. I imagine a little girl, much like my daughter, toddling around in a sweet sundress, or a little boy like my son taking his first steps in a toasty sweater, trying not to fall down. I like to think that each little sweater, hat, or blanket will be passed on to the next child in line, and retired only when it's threadbare.

My son had a favorite sweater that he wore until it was far too short, and many times too tight, but he loved it. Seeing him in that sweater always made me feel proud—something I had made especially for him was so very loved by this little boy that he didn't want to stop wearing it. Although my kids have grown up, I now have the joy of grandchildren. I see them smiling up at me from a handmade blanket or taking those first precarious steps in a favorite sweater.

As you take the time to look through this book and pick out a blanket, sweater, hat, or sundress to make for some little special one in your life, remember you are knitting a gift of love with every stitch. And just maybe there will be a little guy who will want to wear that sweater until it is too small. I hope you have as much fun knitting from this book as I did in designing each piece.

velvet touch

Glowing velvet ribbon adds a touch of glamour to this charming cardigan. Simple eyelet lace surrounds the sweater adding a bit of whimsy. Worked in a warm wool yarn this sweater will be a favorite for keeping her toasty, all winter long. The subtle style of the cardigan works best if the ribbon trim and buttons match the yarn color used.

SIZE
To fit sizes 1 (2, 3, 4) years. Shown in size 1 year.

FINISHED MEASUREMENTS
- Chest (closed) 24 (26, 27½, 29½)" / 61 (66, 70, 75) cm
- Length 12 (13, 14, 15½)" / 30.5 (33, 33.5, 39.5) cm
- Upper arm 10 (11, 12, 13)" / 25 (28, 30, 33) cm

MATERIALS
 4 (5, 5, 6) x 1¾ oz. (50g) balls, each approx. 110 yd. (100.5 m) long, of Classic Elite *Renaissance* (wool) in #7148 Dusk
- Size 8 (5 mm) needles OR SIZE NECESSARY TO OBTAIN CORRECT GAUGE
- 5 x ¾" (2 cm) buttons
- 1 yd. (90 cm) of 12 mm wide Mokuba velvet ribbon #2600 in #27 Plum
- Matching sewing thread
- Stitch holder
- Stitch markers

GAUGE
18 sts and 24 rows = 4" (10 cm) over St st using size 8 (5 mm) needles. BE SURE TO CHECK THE GAUGE.

Cardigan

back
Cast on 50 (54, 58, 62) sts. Work in k2, p2 rib for 1" (2.5 cm), ending with a RS row. P next WS row, inc 4 sts evenly spaced across—54 (58, 62, 66) sts.

EYELET PATTERN
Row 1 K1, ★ k2tog, yo, k2; rep from ★, ending k1.
Row 2 Purl.
Row 3 K3, ★ k2tog, yo, k2; rep from ★, ending last rep, k1 instead of k2.
Row 4 Purl.
Row 5 Rep row 1.
Row 6 Purl.
Then, beg with a k row, cont in St st until piece measures 7 (7½, 8, 9)" / 18 (19, 20.5, 23) cm from beg.

SHAPE ARMHOLES
Bind off 4 sts at beg of next 2 rows—46 (50, 54, 58) sts. Work even until armhole measures 5 (5½, 6, 6½)" / 12.5 (14, 15, 16.5) cm. Bind off.

left front
Cast on 31 (33, 35, 37) sts.
Row 1 (RS) P1 (0, 1, 0), k2 (1, 2, 1), then [p2, k2] 7 (8, 8, 9) times. Cont in k2, p2 rib as established for 1" (2.5 cm), ending with a RS row.
Next row (WS) P2, k2, p2, k1, p to end inc 2 sts evenly spaced across these p sts—33 (35, 37, 39) sts.

EYELET PATTERN

Row 1 (RS) K1 (3, 1, 3), ★ k2tog, yo, k2; rep from ★ 6 (6, 7, 7) times; place marker, k1, p1, k2, p2, k2 (for 8-st band).

Row 2 and all even rows P2, k2, p2, k1, p1 (8-st band); p to end.

Row 3 K3 (1, 3, 1), ★ k2tog, yo, k2; rep from ★, ending last rep k4 instead of k2; work 8-st band.

Row 5 Rep row 1.

DISCONTINUE EYELET BORDER

At this point, cont to work the last 4 sts before 8-st band in eyelet pat as established along with the 8-st band and work rem sts in St st until piece measures 7 (7½, 8, 9)" / 18 (19, 20.5, 23) cm from beg.

SHAPE ARMHOLE

Next row (RS) Bind off 4 sts, work to end—27 (29, 31, 33) sts. Work even until armhole measures 3 (3½, 4, 4½)" / 7.5 (9, 10, 11.5) cm, ending with a RS row.

SHAPE NECK

Next row (WS) Sl 7 sts to a st holder, work to end. Cont to shape neck, binding off 3 sts from neck edge once, dec 1 st every row 5 times. Bind off rem 12 (14, 16, 18) sts for shoulder.

MARK FOR BUTTONHOLES

Place markers for 4 buttons along the center front, the first one ½" (1.5 cm) from lower edge, the top one 2½ (2½, 3, 3½)" / 6.5 (6.5, 7.5, 9) cm from top edge and the others spaced evenly between.

right front

Work as for left front, reversing shaping and band and pat placement and working buttonholes in the p2 ridge opposite markers by k2, yo, p2tog.

sleeves

Cast on 26 (26, 30, 30) sts. Work in k2, p2 rib for 1" (2.5 cm), ending with a RS row. P next WS row, inc 4 sts evenly spaced across—30 (30, 34, 34) sts. Then work the 6-row eyelet pat as on back. Cont in St st inc 1 st each side every 4th row 8 (10, 10, 12) times—46 (50, 54, 58) sts. Work even until piece measures 9 (9, 10, 11)" / 23 (23, 25.5, 28) cm from beg. Bind off.

finishing

Block pieces lightly to measurements, then sew shoulder seams.

NECKBAND AND RIBBON TRIMS

Pick up and k 58 sts evenly around neck edge, including sts from holders. Work in k2, p2 rib for 1" (2.5 cm) forming one more buttonhole on the right front neck to correspond to others. Bind off in rib. Set in sleeves. Sew side and sleeve seams. Sew on buttons. For ribbon trims, cut one 12" (30 cm) length and one 16" (40 cm) length. Pin the longer length to the right shoulder front, overlapping by 1" (2.5 cm) on the back shoulder and pleating the ribbon along the front. Sew in place. Rep for other shoulder. Cut 2 x 10" (25 cm) lengths of ribbon and form bows. Trim bows and sew at shoulder as shown in photo.

all wrapped **up**

Wrap up your precious little bundle in a sweet little sweater and you're ready to go.

Made from ultra soft yarn and worked in seed stitch for a delicate texture, this

sweater is just what the "lullaby set" ordered. Ribbon ties add a finishing touch.

SIZE

To fit sizes 6 (9, 12) months. Shown in size 9 months.

FINISHED MEASUREMENTS

- Chest (wrapped) 21 (23, 24½)" / 53 (58.5, 62) cm
- Length 10 (11, 12½)" / 25.5 (28, 32) cm
- Upper arm 7 (8, 9)" / 18 (20, 23) cm

MATERIALS

- 2 (2, 3) x 1¾ oz. (50g) balls, each approx. 126 yd. (115 m) long, of Berroco *Lullaby* (Tactel/nylon) in #4201 White Magic
- Size 5 (3.75 mm) and 8 (5 mm) needles OR SIZE NECESSARY TO OBTAIN CORRECT GAUGE
- 1 yd. (90 cm) of 4 mm wide Mokuba grosgrain ribbon # 8900 in #97 Lt Pink
- Stitch holders
- Stitch markers

GAUGE

18 sts and 26 rows = 4" (10 cm) over alternating seed st pat using larger needles. BE SURE TO CHECK THE GAUGE.

SIMPLE SEED STITCH PATTERN

Over an odd number of sts.
Row 1 K1, ★ p1, k1; rep from ★ to end.
Row 2 K the purl and p the k sts.
Rep row 2 for simple seed st pat.

ALTERNATING SEED STITCH PATTERN

Over a multiple of 4 sts plus 3.
Row 1 K3, ★ p1, k3; rep from ★ to end.
Row 2 Purl.
Row 3 K1, ★ p1, k3; rep from ★, to end p1, k1.
Row 4 Purl.
Rep rows 1–4 for alternating seed st pat.

Cardigan

back

With smaller needles, cast on 47 (51, 55) sts. Work in simple seed st for 6 rows. Change to larger needles and cont in alternating seed st until piece measures 6½ (7, 8)" / 16.5 (18, 20.5) cm from beg.

SHAPE ARMHOLES

Bind off 4 sts at beg of next 2 rows—39 (43, 47) sts. Work even until armhole measures 3½ (4, 4½)" / 9 (10, 11.5) cm. Bind off.

left front

With smaller needles, cast on 37 (39, 41) sts. Work in simple seed st for 6 rows, inc 1 st on last WS row—38 (40, 42) sts. Change to larger needles.
Next row (RS) Work 32 (34, 36) sts in alternating seed st, pm, work rem 5 sts in simple seed st (for center band). Cont to work the 5-st seed st band and rem sts in alternating seed st until piece measures 4 (4½, 5½)" / 10 (11.5, 14) cm from beg, ending with a RS row.

SHAPE NECK

Next row (WS) Sl 5 sts to a holder, bind off next 3 sts, work to end. Cont to shape neck, dec 1 st from neck edge *every* row 4 times, every other row 4 (5, 6) times, every 4th row 4 times—12 (14, 16) sts rem. Work even until same length as back to shoulder. Bind off.

right front

Work as for left front, reversing all shaping and band placement.

sleeves

With smaller needles, cast on 27 sts. Work in simple seed st for 6 rows. Change to larger needles and cont in alternating seed st inc 1 st each side every 4th row 4 (6, 8) times—35 (39, 43) sts. Work even until piece measures 6½ (7½, 8½)" / 16.5 (19, 21.5) cm from beg. Bind off.

finishing

Do not block pieces. Sew shoulder seams. Set in sleeves. Sew side and sleeve seams.

NECKBAND

With smaller needles, pick up and k 95 sts evenly around neck edge, including sts on holders. Work in simple seed st for 1" (2.5 cm). Bind off in pat. Cut ribbons into 4 x 9" (23 cm) lengths. From WS, sew 1 ribbon to top of right front edge, and 1 to bottom of right front edge. Then, sew 2 more ribbons to correspond on RS of the left front, 2 sts in from side seam.

baby bear

Soft and snugly, here is the perfect companion to take to dreamland. Every baby loves a plush little bear to grab onto and make friends with and this one comes with a sweater to match baby's own. How cute is that!

FINISHED MEASUREMENTS
Height 15" (38 cm)

MATERIALS
 2 x 1¾ oz. (50 g) balls, each approx. 90 yd. (82 m) long, of Berroco *Plush* (nylon) in #1901 Crema
- Small amount of black yarn
- Sizes 6 (4 mm) and 9 (5.5 mm) needles OR SIZE NECESSARY TO OBTAIN CORRECT GAUGE
- 5 oz. (125 g) polyester stuffing
- Stitch markers
- Tapestry needle

GAUGE
16 sts and 20 rows = 4" (10 cm) BE SURE TO CHECK THE GAUGE.

NOTE The bear is worked from the neck down, then the head is worked from the neck up.

knitting tip When knitting toys and clothes for children, whenever possible, use a yarn that can be machine washed.

Bear

neck
With smaller needles, cast on 16 sts, k3 rows. Change to larger needles.
Row 1 K2, pm, k6, pm, k2, pm, k6.
Rows 2 and all even rows Purl.
Row 3 Inc in first st, inc 1 st in next st, sl marker, inc 1 st in next st, k4, inc 1 st in next st, sl marker, inc 1 st in each of next 2 sts, sl marker, inc 1st in next st, k4, inc 1 st in last st—24 sts.
Rows 5, 7, 9, 11 Inc 1 st in first and last st of row; *k to 1 st before each marker, [inc in next st; slip marker, inc in next st] rep from * across—(56 sts on Row 11).
Row 12 Purl.

SHAPE ARMS
* K across 12 sts; turn. Working on 12 sts for arm only, work in St st until piece measures 4" (10 cm), ending with a p row.
Next row K2 tog across—6 sts.
Fasten off, leaving long piece of yarn. Thread needle with long strand of yarn, pull though all sts on needle, draw up tightly and fasten. Sew seams. Rejoin yarn and work across 16 sts for body; then rep from * for 2nd arm shaping.

shape body
Rejoin yarn and k across rem 16 sts of body; turn, p across all sts—32 sts. Work even in St st until piece measures 7" (18 cm) from neck beg. Bind off all sts.

head

NOTE Seam will be down one side of head.
With RS facing, pick up and k 16 sts across neck sts. Turn. Purl, inc 8 sts evenly spaced—24 sts. Turn.
Row 1 K1, inc in next st, k7, [inc in next st] twice, k4, inc in next st; place marker, inc in next st, k4, inc in next st, k2—30 sts.
Row 2 and all even rows Purl.
Row 3 K1, inc in next st, k9, [inc in next st] twice, k to 1 st before marker, inc in next st, slip marker, inc in next st, k to last st, inc in last st—36 sts.
Rows 5, 7, 9 K to 1 st before marker, [inc 1 st, slip marker, inc 1 st] k to end—42 sts on Row 9.
Row 11 K to 4 sts before marker, [k2tog] twice, slip marker, [k2tog] twice, k to end.
Rows 13, 15 K to 2 st before marker (k2tog, slip marker, k2tog), k to end.
Row 17 K1, k2tog, k10, [k2tog] twice, k to 2 sts before marker [k2tog, slip marker, k2tog] k to last 2 sts; k2tog.
Row 19 K1, [k2tog] across.
Row 21 K2tog across. Fasten off, leaving a long piece of yarn. Thread needle with long strand of yarn, pull through all sts on needle, draw up tightly and fasten. Sew side seam of head.
Stuff head with polyester stuffing, taking care to put extra stuffing for nose shaping. Stuff arms. Sew rem back seam and down side. Stuff body, with extra padding at the front for the tummy.

legs (make 2)
Cast on 14 sts. Work in St st until piece measures 4½" (11.5 cm) from beg, ending with a p row.

SHAPE FEET
Row 1 K8, inc in each of the next 4 sts; k to end.
Rows 2, 4, 6, 8 Purl.
Row 3 K10, inc in each of the next 4 sts; k to end.
Row 5 K10 [k2tog] 5 times; k to end.
Row 7 K8, [k2tog] 4 times; k to end.
Bind off all sts. Sew leg seam. Stuff, shaping feet to fit the knitted shape. Sew top tog of each leg. Placing side of leg into side edge of body, baste carefully into place, then sew. Sew small remaining opening between legs.

ears (make 2)
Cast on 7 sts, k3 rows, p1 row. Bind off all sts in k, leaving long end for sewing. Weaving long end across bound-off sts, pull up to gather and make garter st edge curve. Baste in place on each side of head (using seam for a guide), fastening from garter st edge down side, across bottom, and to other garter st edge. Sew in place.

finishing
With black yarn, embroider eyes, nose, and mouth as shown in photo.

baby bear's cardigan

This baby bear sports a miniature version of the All Wrapped Up cardigan. Baby Bear's cardigan is knit in the same supersoft machine-washable wool. Why not knit the top in blue or green for a cute baby boy bear, or in colors to match your nursery? Change the ribbon colors to match the new yarn colors to keep the contemporary style.

SIZE

To fit a bear 16" (40 cm) long, with 12" (30.5 cm) chest, as shown.

FINISHED MEASUREMENTS

- Chest (wrapped) 14" (35.5 cm)
- Length 6½" (16.5 cm)
- Upper arm 6" (15 cm)

MATERIALS

 1 x 1¾ oz. (50 g) ball, approx. 126 yd. (115 m) long, of Berroco *Lullaby* (Tactel/nylon) in #4205 Girlie Girl

- Size 5 (3.75 mm) and 8 (5 mm) needles OR SIZE NECESSARY TO OBTAIN CORRECT GAUGE
- 1 yd. (9 cm) of ¼" (6 mm) wide ribbon
- Stitch holders

GAUGE

18 sts and 26 rows = 4" (10 cm) over alternating seed st pat using larger needles. BE SURE TO CHECK THE GAUGE.

SIMPLE SEED STITCH

Over an odd number of sts.
Row 1 K1, ★ p1, k1; rep from ★ to end.
Row 2 K the purl and p the k sts.
Rep row 2 for simple seed st pat.

ALTERNATING SEED STITCH

Over a multiple of 4 sts plus 3.
Row 1 K3, ★ p1, k3; rep from ★ to end.
Row 2 Purl.
Row 3 K1, ★ p1, k3; rep from ★, ending p1, k1.
Row 4 Purl.
Rep rows 1–4 for alternating seed st pat.

Cardigan

back

With smaller needles, cast on 31 sts. Work in simple seed st for 5 rows. Change to larger needles and cont in alternating seed st until piece measures 3½" (9 cm) from beg.

SHAPE ARMHOLES

Bind off 2 sts at beg of next 2 rows—27 sts. Work even until armhole measures 3" (7.5 cm). Bind off.

left front

With smaller needles, cast on 21 sts. Work in simple seed st for 5 rows, inc 1 st on last row—22 sts. Change to larger needles.
Next row (WS) Work 3 sts in simple seed st, purl to end. Cont to work the last 3 sts of RS rows in simple seed st (for front band) and rem 19 sts in alternating seed st until piece measures 2½" (6.5 cm) from beg, ending with a RS row.

SHAPE NECK

Next row (WS) Sl 3 sts to a holder, bind off next 2 sts, work to end. Cont to shape neck dec 1 st at neck edge *every* row 3 times, then every other row twice, then every 4th row 3 times—7 sts. Work even until same length as back to shoulder. Bind off.

right front

Work as for left front, reversing all shaping and also the band placement.

sleeves

With smaller needles, cast on 25 sts. Work in simple seed st for 5 rows. Change to larger needles and cont in alternating seed st until piece measures 2" (5 cm) from beg. Bind off.

finishing

Do not block pieces. Sew shoulder seams. Set in sleeves. Sew side and sleeve seams.

NECKBAND

With smaller needles pick up and k 63 sts around entire neck edge, including sts from holders. Work in simple seed st for 5 rows. Bind off in pat. Cut ribbons into 4 x 7" (18 cm) lengths. From WS, sew one ribbon to top of right front edge, one to bottom of right front edge. Then sew 2 more ribbons to correspond on RS of the left front, 2 sts in from side seam.

stripe **it rich**

The little man in your life will look adorable in this bright pullover. Reverse stockinette stitch adds oodles of texture, and gives the stripes extra dimension—but still allows this to be a very easy project. So pick up those needles and get started on this fast and colorful pullover that's bound to become a firm favorite.

SIZE
To fit 6 (9, 12, 18) months. Shown in 9 months size.

FINISHED MEASUREMENTS
- Chest 24 (26, 28, 30)" / 61 (66, 71, 76) cm
- Length 11 (12, 13½, 15½)" / 28 (30.5, 34, 39.5) cm
- Upper arm 8½ (9½, 10½, 11½)" / 21.5 (24, 26.5, 29) cm

MATERIALS
- 1 x 6 oz. (170 g) skein, approx. 330 yd. (302 m) long, of Caron *Simply Soft* (acrylic) in #9747 Iris (A), #9702 Off White (C), and #9748 Rubine Red (D)
- 1 x 6 oz. (170 g) skein, approx 330 yd. (302 m) long, of Caron *Simply Soft Brites* (acrylic) in #9609 Berry Blue (B)
- Size 8 (5 mm) needles OR SIZE NECESSARY TO OBTAIN CORRECT GAUGE
- 3 x ⅜" (1 cm) buttons

GAUGE
16 sts and 24 rows = 4" (10 cm) over reverse St st and stripe pat using size 8 (5 mm) needles. BE SURE TO CHECK THE GAUGE.

STRIPE PATTERN
Working in reverse St st, work 4 rows A, 4 rows B, 1 row C, 2 rows D, 1 row C. Rep these 12 rows for stripe pat.
NOTE The purl side is the RS of work.

Sweater

back
With A, cast on 50 (54, 58, 62) sts. Work in k1, p1 rib for 1" (2.5 cm). Cont in reverse St st and stripe pat until piece measures 7 (7½, 8½, 10)" / 18 (19, 21.5, 25.5) cm from beg.

SHAPE ARMHOLES
Bind off 5 sts at beg of next 2 rows—40 (44, 48, 52) sts. Work even until armhole measures 4 (4½, 5, 5½)" / 10 (11.5, 12.5, 14) cm. Bind off.

front
Work as for back until armhole measures 1½ (2, 3, 3½)" / 4 (5, 7.5, 9) cm.

SHAPE NECK
Next row (RS) Work 17 (19, 20, 21) sts, join a 2nd ball of yarn and bind off center 6 (6, 8, 10) sts, work to end.
Working both sides at once, bind off 2 sts from each neck edge 3 times—11 (13, 14, 15) sts rem each side. When same length as back, bind off rem sts each side from shoulders.

sleeves
With A, cast on 28 (28, 30, 30) sts. Work in k1, p1 rib for 1" (2.5 cm). Then cont in reverse St st and stripe pat inc 1 st each side every 6th (4th, 4th, 4th) row 3 (5, 6, 8) times—34 (38, 42, 46) sts. Work even

in stripe pat until piece measures 6 (6, 6½, 7)" /
15 (15, 16.5, 18) cm from beg. Bind off.

finishing
Sew right shoulder seam.

LEFT FRONT BUTTONHOLE BAND
With A, pick up and k 11 (13, 14, 15) sts along the
left front shoulder. Work in k1, p1 rib for 32 rows.
Bind off. It is not necessary to work buttonholes as
the sts are loose enough and the buttons small
enough to pull through the sts.

NECKBAND
Pick up sts as foll: 4 sts along the left front neck
band, 25 (25, 27, 29) sts from front neck edge,
29 (31, 34, 37) sts along the back neck and
shoulder edge. Work in k1, p1 rib for 3 rows.
Bind off. Sew on 3 buttons to left back shoulder
and button shoulder closed. Set in sleeves. Sew side
and sleeve seams.

bow **tied**

Just like a perfect little present this cardigan is wrapped up with a bow. Knit it up quickly in a delicious berry colored cotton blend yarn, or a color of your choice. Delicate picot edging adds a decidedly girlie touch. This sturdy little cardigan can go straight from the playground to a party.

SIZE
To fit 1 (2, 3, 4) years. Shown in 2 years size.

FINISHED MEASUREMENTS
- Chest (closed) 24 (27, 28½, 30)" / 61 (68.5, 72, 76) cm
- Length 12½ (13½, 14½, 15½)" / 31.5 (34.5, 36.5, 39.5) cm
- Upper arm 9½ (10½, 11½, 12½)" / 25 (28, 30, 33) cm

MATERIALS
 7 (7, 8, 8) x 1¾ oz. (50 g) balls, each approx. 98 yd. (90 m) long, of Rowan *All Seasons Cotton* (cotton/acrylic) in #211 Blackcurrant
- Size 8 (5 mm) needles OR SIZE NECESSARY TO OBTAIN CORRECT GAUGE
- 1 yd. (90 cm) of 32 mm wide Mokuba ruffled satin ribbon #4895 in #39 Apricot
- Matching thread
- 5 x ⅝" (1.5 cm) buttons

GAUGE
18 sts and 22 rows = 4" (10 cm) over St st using size 8 (5 mm) needles. BE SURE TO CHECK THE GAUGE.

Cardigan

back
Cast on 54 (60, 64, 68) sts. K1 row, p1 row.
Next (eyelet) row (RS) ★ K2tog, yo; rep from ★, ending k2. Then beg with a p row, cont in St st until the piece measures 7½ (8, 8½, 9)" / 19 (20.5, 21.5, 23) cm from the eyelet row.

SHAPE ARMHOLES
Bind off 4 (5, 5, 5) sts at beg of next 2 rows—46 (50, 54, 58) sts. Work even until armhole measures 5 (5½, 6, 6½)" / 12.5 (14, 15, 16.5) cm. Bind off.

left front
Cast on 25 (28, 30, 32) sts. Work first 3 rows as on back. Then, beg with a p row, work in St st until piece measures 7½ (8, 8½, 9)" / 19 (20.5, 21.5, 23) cm from the eyelet row.

SHAPE ARMHOLE
Next row (RS) Bind off 4 (5, 5, 5) sts, work to end—21 (23, 25, 27) sts. Work even until armhole measures 2 (2½, 3, 3½)" / 5 (6.5, 7.5, 9) cm, ending with a RS row.

SHAPE NECK
Next row (WS) Bind off 4 (5, 5, 5) sts, work to end. Cont to shape neck binding off 2 sts at neck edge 3 times more—12 (13, 15, 17) sts rem.

Work even until same length as back to shoulder. Bind off.

right front

Work as for left front, reversing shaping.

sleeves

Cast on 28 (28, 30, 30) sts. Work first 3 rows as on back. Then, beg with a p row, work in St st inc 1 st each side every 4th row 7 (10, 11, 13) times— 42 (48, 52, 56) sts. Work even until piece measures 9 (11, 12, 12½)" / 23 (28, 30.5, 32) cm from beg. Bind off.

finishing

Block pieces lightly to measurements. Sew shoulder seams. Set in sleeves. Sew side and sleeve seams. Turn up hem at eyelet rows and sew to WS.

LEFT AND RIGHT FRONT BAND

Pick up and k 47 (53, 57, 59) sts along left front edge. Work in k1, p1 rib for 1" (2.5 cm). Bind off. Place markers for 5 buttons along band, the first one at ½" (1.5 cm) from lower edge, the top one 2" (5 cm) from top edge, and the others evenly spaced between. Work right front band to correspond to left, working a yo, k2tog to correspond to each button marker on left front in the 2nd row.

NECK BAND AND TRIMS

Pick up and k 61 (65, 65, 65) sts evenly around neck edge. Work in k1, p1 rib for 1" (2.5 cm), working 1 more buttonhole on the right front neck in the 2nd row of rib. Bind off. Sew on buttons. Attach ribbon by first pinning a length at 1" (2.5 cm) down from armhole beg and end at the center front. Baste and sew in place. Cut a 9" (23 cm) length of ribbon and seam ends tog to form a circle for the bow. Cut a 2nd length of ribbon and pleat to 2½" (6.5 cm) to sew around the center of the bow. Baste and sew in place on the right front band with the pleated center up to the edge of the right band.

bright light

Bright yellow adds a cheerful note to this pair of booties and hat with just a touch of white for accent. If you've never tried felting before this is a great first project. The hat and booties are worked in one piece and sewn together, so you don't have to worry about working in the round.

SIZE
To fit 3–6 months (6–9 months). Shown in size 3–6 months.

FINISHED MEASUREMENTS
HAT (AFTER FELTING)
● Head circumference 18 (19)" / 45.5 (48) cm
● Depth 6½" (16.5 cm) with edge rolled
BOOTIES
● Sole length 3½ (4½)" / 9 (11.5) cm

MATERIALS
● 1 x 3½ oz. (100 g) skein, approx. 220 yd. (201 m) long, of Cascade Yarns *Cascade 220* (wool) in #4147 Yellow (A), and #8505 White (B)
● Size 8 (5.5 mm) needles OR SIZE NECESSARY TO OBTAIN CORRECT GAUGE

GAUGE
18 sts and 24 rows = 4" (10 cm) over St st using size 8 (5.5 mm) needles before felting. BE SURE TO CHECK THE GAUGE.

Hat

With B, cast on 60 (66) sts. Work in St st for 2" (5 cm). Work 2 rows in St st with A, 2 rows with B, then cont with A only until piece measures 6½" (16.5 cm) from beg.
Dec row 1 (RS) [K4, k2tog] 10 (11) times—50 (55) sts.
Rows 2, 4, 6 and 8 Purl.
Row 3 [K3, k2tog] 10 (11) times—40 (44) sts.
Row 5 [K2, k2tog] 10 (11) times—30 (33) sts.
Row 7 [K1, k2tog] 10 (11) times—20 (22) sts.
Row 9 [K2tog] 10 (11) times—10 (11) sts.
Cut yarn leaving a long end.

finishing
Pull through rem sts tightly twice and draw up tightly to finish top. Sew back seam.

Booties

With B, cast on 18 (24) sts. K1 row.
Row 2 K1, yo to M1, k7 (10), [yo, k1] twice, yo, k 7 (10), yo, k1.
Rows 3, 5, 7, 9 and 11 Knit; always k into back lp of each yo.
Row 4 K2, yo, k7 (10), yo, k2, yo, k3, yo, k 7 (10), yo, k2.
Row 6 K3, yo, k7 (10), [yo, k4] twice, yo, k7 (10), yo, k3.

Row 8 K4, yo, k7 (10), yo, k5, yo, k6, yo, k7 (10), yo, k4.

Row 10 K5, yo, k7 (10), [yo, k7] twice, yo, k7 (10), yo, k5—43 (49) sts.

Change to A and work in St st for 6 rows.

shape instep

Row 1 (RS) K 24 (26), sk2p, turn.

Row 2 Sl 1, p 5 (7), p3tog, turn.

Row 3 Sl 1, k 5 (7), sk2p, turn.

Rows 4–9 [Rep rows 2 and 3] 3 times.

Row 10 Rep row 2.

Row 11 Sl 1, k5 (7), skp, k to end of row.

Row 12 Sl 1, p5 (7), p2tog, p to end of row— 21 (27) sts. Then cont in St st, work 4 rows A, 2 rows B, 2 rows A, 6 rows B. Bind off. Sew back and sole seam.

Felting process

Set washing machine to low water cycle, hot wash/cold rinse setting. Add small amount of mild detergent and run through one cycle. Repeat until desired felting is achieved (see page 105–6).

spice girl

What toddler wouldn't love a lacy poncho in a bright spicy color, with just enough warmth to chase away a little chill but still light and delicate. Worked in two straight pieces in simple lace stitch, your little "spice girl" will be ready in a jiffy to show off her talents. No shaping makes for an easy starter project.

SIZE
One size to fit size 2–4 years.

FINISHED MEASUREMENTS
RECTANGLES
- Width 11" (28 cm)
- Length 19½" (49.5 cm)

MATERIALS
 1 x 6 oz. (170 g) skein, approx. 330 yd. (300 m) long, of Caron *Simply Soft Brites* (acrylic) in #9603 Papaya
- Size 8 (5 mm) needles OR SIZE NECESSARY TO OBTAIN CORRECT GAUGE
- Stitch markers

GAUGE
16 sts and 24 rows = 4" (10 cm) over lace pat st using size 8 (5 mm) needles. BE SURE TO CHECK THE GAUGE.

Poncho

rectangle (make 2)
Cast on 44 sts.
Row 1 (RS) K3 (for border), k2, ★ yo, k2, skp, k2tog, k2, yo, k1; rep from ★, ending k3 (for border).
Rows 2 and 4 K3, p38 , k3.
Row 3 K3 (for border), k1, ★ yo, k2, skp, k2tog, k2, yo, k1; rep from ★, ending k2 instead of k1, k3 (for border).
Row 5 K3, p38, k3.
Row 6 Rep row 5.
Rep 1–6 for pat st until piece measures 19½" (49.5 cm). Bind off knitwise.

finishing
Match the bound-off edge of the 2nd rectangle to fit across the first 11" (28 cm) of the side edge of the first rectangle. Sew the pieces tog. Match the bound-off edge of the first rectangle to the first 11" (28 cm) of the side edge of the 2nd rectangle, and sew tog, closing up the neck.

vested interest

Perfect for just a little warmth, a vest can be a great addition to any toddler's wardrobe. This pattern includes one of the best ways to add color and charm without too much time or difficulty. We love the basic slip stitch—it creates a color pattern that looks much harder to knit than it really is.

SIZE

To fit 6 (9, 12, 18) months. Shown in size 9 months.

FINISHED MEASUREMENTS

- Chest 21½ (23, 24½, 26)" / 54.5 (58.5, 62, 66) cm
- Length 12 (12½, 13½, 14½)" / 30.5 (32, 34, 37) cm

MATERIALS

1 x 6 oz. (170 g) skein, approx. 330 yd. (300 m) long, of Caron *Simply Soft* (acrylic) in #9707 Dark Sage (A), #9705 Sage (B)
- 1 x 6 oz. (170 g) skein, approx. 330 yd. (300 m) long, of Caron *Simply Soft Brites* (acrylic) in #9609 Berry Blue (C)
- Size 8 (5 mm) needles OR SIZE NECESSARY TO OBTAIN CORRECT GAUGE
- Safety pin

GAUGE

18 sts and 32 rows = 4" (10 cm) over slip stitch pattern using size 8 (5 mm) needles. BE SURE TO CHECK THE GAUGE.

fashion tip This vest would look great worked in any color combination. Why not make one in bright pinks or citrus colors for your favorite tomboy?

SLIP STITCH PATTERN

Over a multiple of 3 sts plus 1.
Rows 1 and 2 With A, knit.
Row 3 With B, sl 1 wyib, ★ k2, sl 1 wyib; rep from ★ to end.
Row 4 ★ Wyif, sl 1, yarn to back and k2; rep from ★, ending wyif, sl 1.
Rows 5 and 6 With A, knit.
Row 7 Rep row 3.
Row 8 Rep row 4.
Rows 9 and 10 With A, knit.
Row 11 With C, rep row 3.
Row 12 With C, rep row 4.
Rep rows 1–12 for slip stitch pat.

Vest

back

With A, cast on 56 (60, 64, 66) sts. Work in k1, p1 rib for 1½" (4 cm), dec 7 (8, 9, 8) sts evenly spaced across last WS row—49 (52, 55, 58) sts. Work even in slip stitch pat until piece measures 7½ (7½, 8, 8½)" / 19 (19, 20.5, 21.5) cm from beg.

SHAPE ARMHOLES

Bind off 4 sts at beg of next 2 rows—41 (44, 47, 50) sts. Work even until armhole measures 4½ (5, 5½, 6)" / 11.5 (12.5, 14, 15) cm. Bind off.

front

Work as for back (including armhole shaping)
until armhole measures ½ (1, 1, 1)" / 1.5 (2.5,
2.5, 2.5) cm.

SHAPE V NECK

Next row (RS) Work 20 (21, 23, 24) sts, place
center 1 (2, 1, 2) sts on a safety pin, join a 2nd ball
of yarn and work rem 20 (21, 23, 24) sts. Working
both sides at once, dec 1 st from each neck edge
every other row 10 times—10 (11, 13, 14) sts rem
each side. When front is same length as back, bind
off sts each side for shoulders.

finishing

Sew left shoulder seam. With A, pick up and k 21
(22, 21, 22) sts from back neck, 17 (17, 19, 21) sts
from left neck edge, 1 (2, 1, 2) sts from safety pin,
17 (17, 19, 21) sts from right neck edge. Work in
k1, p1 rib for 3 rows, dec 1 st each side of center
V-neck sts every other row twice. Bind off. Sew
other shoulder. With A, pick up and k 42 (46, 50,
54) sts around each armhole. Work 3 rows in k1,
p1 rib. Bind off. Sew side seams.

cable gram

You'll be getting rave reviews from far and wide with this special little cardigan, worked in "oh so soft" cotton and wool blend yarn that will glide through your fingers as you work the delicate cables. For a finishing touch, a pleated ribbon graces the front and bottom of the sweater.

SIZE

To fit 1 (2) years. Shown in size 1 year.

FINISHED MEASUREMENTS

- Chest 23 (27)" / 58.5 (68.5) cm
- Length 12 (14)" / 30.5 (35.5) cm
- Upper arm 9 (10)" / 23 (25.5) cm

MATERIALS

- 6 (7) x 1¾ oz. (50 g) balls, each approx. 123 yd. (112 m) long, of Rowan *Wool Cotton* (wool/cotton) in #941 Clear
- Size 5 (3.75 mm) and 6 (4 mm) needles OR SIZE NECESSARY TO OBTAIN CORRECT GAUGE
- Cable needles (cn)
- 1 yd. (90 cm) of 15 mm wide Mokuba pleated ribbon #4488 in #12 Ivory
- Matching thread
- 5 x ⅝" (15 mm) buttons

GAUGE

32 sts and 24 rows = 4" (10 cm) over cable pat using larger needles. BE SURE TO CHECK THE GAUGE.

fashion tip If knitting this cardigan for an extra special occasion, add ribbon trim to the cuffs as well.

CABLE PATTERN

Over a multiple of 8 sts.
Row 1 P1, k6, ★ p2, k6; rep from ★, ending p1.
Row 2 and all even rows K the knit and p the purl sts.
Rows 3 and 5 Rep row 1.
Row 7 P1, ★ sl 3 sts to cn and hold to front, k3, k3 from cn, (6-st cable), p2; rep from ★, ending 6-st cable, p1.
Row 8 Rep row 2.
Rep rows 1–8 for cable pat.

Cardigan

body

With smaller needle, cast on 176 (208) sts. Work in k2, p2 rib for 4 rows. Change to larger needles, and cont in cable pat until piece measures 7½ (9)" / 19 (23) cm from beg.

SEPARATE AT ARMHOLES

Next row (RS) Work 32 (40) sts (right front), join a 2nd ball of yarn and bind off 16 sts, work until there are 80 (96) sts on needle (back), bind off next 16 sts, work to end—32 (40) sts for left front.

left front

Work on the left front sts only, work even until piece measures 2 (2½)" / 5 (6.5) cm from armhole bind-off, ending with a RS row.

SHAPE NECK

Next row (WS) Bind off 5 sts, work to end. Cont to shape neck, binding off 2 sts from neck edge once, then dec 1 st every row 5 times—20 (28) sts. Work even until armhole measures 4½ (5)" / 11.5 (12.5) cm. Bind off sts for shoulder.

back

Return to the 80 (96) sts for back and work even until piece measures 4½ (5)" / 11.5 (12.5) cm from armhole bind-off. Bind off all sts.

right front

Work as for left front, reversing all shaping.

sleeves

With smaller needles cast on 40 (44) sts. Work in k2, p2 rib for 4 rows. Change to larger needles and cont in cable pat inc 1 st each side (working incs in cable pat twists when there are sufficient sts) every 2nd row 8 times, every 4th row 8 (10) times—72 (80) sts. Work even until piece measures 9 (11)" / 23 (28) cm from beg. Bind off.

finishing

Sew shoulder seams. Set sleeves in armhole. Sew side and sleeve seams.

LEFT FRONT BAND

With smaller needles, pick up and k 62 (74) sts along the left front edge. Work in k2, p2 rib for 4 rows, bind off in rib. Place markers for 4 buttons along the band, the first one ½" (1.5 cm) from lower edge, the last one 2½ (2¾)" / 6.5 (7) cm from top edge, and the others spaced evenly between.

RIGHT FRONT BAND

Work right front band to correspond to left front band, working buttonholes opposite markers by yo, k2tog.

NECKBAND

With smaller needles, pick up and k 78 sts evenly around neck edge. Work in k2, p2 rib for 4 rows, forming 1 more buttonhole on the 2nd row opposite the others on right front neck. Bind off in rib. Sew on buttons. Sew trim onto lower edge and onto right front band.

two by two

Worked in a double moss stitch with a "two by two" ribbing, this cotton pullover will give your little one double the pleasure. Slip it on with shorts, a skirt, or sundress, and it's sure to become a versatile addition to any wardrobe. Work in a variation color too, so that your little girl can always wear her favorite top.

SIZE

To fit sizes 1 (2, 3, 4) years. Shown in size 2 years.

FINISHED MEASUREMENTS

- Chest 24 (26, 28, 30)" / 61 (66, 71, 76) cm
- Length 10 (11, 12½, 14)" / 25.5 (28, 32, 35.5) cm
- Upper arm 8 (9, 10, 11)" / 20.5 (23, 25.5, 28) cm

MATERIALS

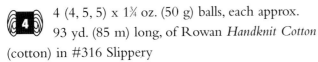 4 (4, 5, 5) x 1¾ oz. (50 g) balls, each approx. 93 yd. (85 m) long, of Rowan *Handknit Cotton* (cotton) in #316 Slippery
- Size 6 (4 mm) needles OR SIZE NECESSARY TO OBTAIN CORRECT GAUGE.
- Safety pin

GAUGE

16 sts and 26 rows = 4" (10 cm) over double seed st using size 6 (4 mm) needles. BE SURE TO CHECK THE GAUGE.

DOUBLE SEED STITCH PATTERN

Over a multiple of 4 sts.
Row 1 (RS) ★ K2, p2; rep from ★ to end.
Rows 2 and 4 K the knit and p the purl sts.
Row 3 ★ P2, k2; rep from ★ to end.
Rep rows 1–4 for double seed st pat.

Top

back

Cast on 48 (52, 56, 60) sts. Work in k2, p2 rib for ¾" (2 cm). Cont in double seed st pat until piece measures 6 (6½, 7½, 8½)" / 15 (16.5, 19, 21.5) cm from beg.

SHAPE ARMHOLE

Bind off 4 sts at beg of next 2 rows—40 (44, 48, 52) sts. Work even until armhole measures 4 (4½, 5, 5½)" / 10 (11.5, 12.5, 14) cm. Bind off.

front

Work as for back until armhole measures 2 (2½, 3, 3½)" / 5 (6.5, 7.5, 9) cm.

NECK SHAPING

Next row (RS) Work 19 (21, 23, 25) sts, place center 2 sts on a safety pin, join a 2nd ball of yarn and work to end. Working both sides at once, dec 1 st each side of next edge every row 8 (9, 10, 10) times—11 (12, 13, 15) sts rem each side. Work even until same number of rows as back. Bind off sts each side for shoulders.

sleeves

Cast on 28 (28, 30, 30) sts. Work in k2, p2 rib for ¾" (2 cm). Cont in double seed st pat inc 1 st each side of next row then every 4th row 2 (4, 5, 7) times more—34 (38, 42, 46) sts. Work even until piece

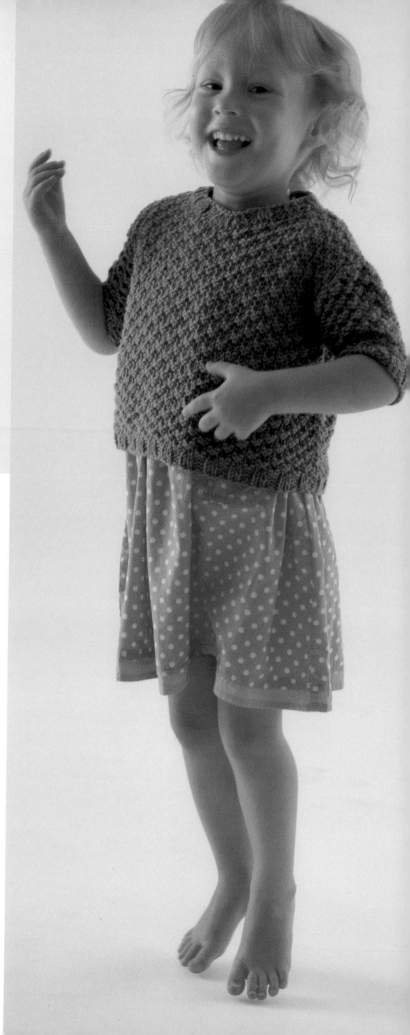

measures 4 (4½, 4½, 5½)" / 10 (11.5, 11.5, 14) cm
from beg. Bind off.

finishing
Sew left shoulder seam.

NECKBAND
Pick up and k 52 (56, 60, 60) sts evenly around
neck edge including the 2 knit sts on safety pin.
Work in k2, p2 rib for 3 rows dec 1 st each side
of 2 center k sts every other row twice. Bind off.
Sew right shoulder seam. Set in sleeves. Sew side
and sleeve seams.

fashion tip Add blanket stitches in a
contrast color around the bottom edge
to personalize this classic sweater.

blue wave

Watercolors gently move across this blanket evoking the beauty of a tranquil ocean. The slip stitch allows the blanket to lie flat, and the variegated yarn changes pattern as the stitches slip by. Satin blanket binding adds a soft finishing touch for little fingers to caress. Made in an easy care washable acrylic yarn.

FINISHED MEASUREMENTS
- Length 38" (96.5 cm)
- Width 32" (81 cm)

MATERIALS

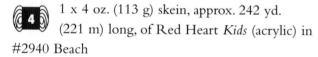 1 x 4 oz. (113 g) skein, approx. 242 yd. (221 m) long, of Red Heart *Kids* (acrylic) in #2940 Beach
- Size 13 (9 mm) circular needle, 24" (60 cm) long OR SIZE NECESSARY TO OBTAIN CORRECT GAUGE
- 1 package light blue satin blanket binding
- Matching thread

GAUGE

18 sts and 24 rows = 4" (10 cm) over woven pat st using size 13 (9 mm) needles. BE SURE TO CHECK THE GAUGE.

WOVEN PATTERN STITCH

Over an even number of sts.
Row 1 ★ K1, bring yarn to front and sl next st, bring yarn to back; rep from ★ to end.
Row 2 ★ P1, bring yarn to back and sl next st, bring yarn to front; rep from ★ to end.
Rep rows 1 and 2 for woven pat st.

Blanket

Cast on 144 sts. Work in woven pat st for 38" (96.5 cm). Bind off.

finishing

Block the blanket lightly to measurements. Fold satin binding in half all around outer corners, to cover the edges, and miter at the corners. Sew in place invisibly with matching thread.

finishing tip If you spend a lot of time knitting something large like this blanket, do not be tempted to rush the finishing. Here, mitered corners and invisible stitching are used on the satin binding to complete the project with neat edges.

fair isle friend

What little guy wouldn't love to toddle around in a warm winter sweater and hat? Perfect for playtime they are both durable and stylish so your boy can be the leader of the pack. Worked in just three colors, this Fair Isle knit will be done before you know it. A two button band at the neck makes it easy to get on and off.

SIZE

SWEATER
To fit 9 months (24 months). Shown in size 9 months.

HAT
To fit 9–12 months. Shown in 9–12 months size.

FINISHED MEASUREMENTS

SWEATER
- Chest 24 (28)" / 61 (71) cm
- Length 12½ (14½)" / 32 (37) cm
- Upper arm 9 (10)" / 23 (26) cm

HAT
- Head circumference 18" (45.5 cm)
- Depth 7" (18 cm)

MATERIALS

SWEATER
4 (5) x 3½ oz. (100 g) skeins, each approx. 132 yd. (120.5 m) long, of Cascade *Pastaza* (llama/wool) in #026 Beige (MC)
- 1 x 3½ oz. (100 g) skein, approx. 132 yd. (120.5 m) long, of Cascade *Pastaza* (llama/wool) in #072 Brown (A), and #1107 Blue (B)

HAT
- 1 x 3½ oz. (100 g) skein, approx. 132 yd. (120.5 m) long, of Cascade *Pastaza* (llama/wool) in #026 Beige (MC), #072 Brown (A), and #1107 Blue (B)

YOU WILL ALSO NEED
- Size 9 (5.5 mm) needles OR SIZE NECESSARY TO OBTAIN CORRECT GAUGE
- Size I/9 (5.5 mm) crochet hook
- 2 x ⅝" (15 mm) buttons
- Stitch holders

GAUGE
16 sts and 20 rows = 4" (10 cm) over St st using size 9 (5.5 mm) needles. BE SURE TO CHECK THE GAUGE.

Sweater

back
With MC, cast on 48 (56) sts. Work in k1, p1 rib for 1½" (4 cm). Then cont in St st for 2 rows.

CHART PAT
NOTE For color chart, see page 57.
Next row (RS) Work row 1 of chart 8-st rep a total of 6 (7) times. Cont to foll chart through row 19. Then cont in St st with MC only until piece measures 8 (9½)" / 20.5 (24) cm from beg.

SHAPE ARMHOLES
Bind off 4 sts at beg of next 2 rows—40 (48) sts. Work even until armhole measures 4½ (5)" / 11.5 (12.5) cm. Bind off.

front

Work as for back through the armhole shaping. Work 0 (2) rows even in St st.

SEPARATE FOR NECK

Next row (RS) Work 17 (21) sts, join a 2nd ball of yarn and bind off center 6 sts, work to end. Work both sides at once until placket opening measures 1¾" (4.5 cm).

SHAPE NECK

For each neck edge bind off 2 (3) sts once, dec 1 st every other row 3 times—12 (15) sts rem each side. When same length as back, bind off sts each side for shoulders.

sleeves

Cast on 24 sts. Work in k1, p1 rib for 1½" (4 cm). Then cont in St st for 2 rows.

CHART PAT

Next row (RS) Work row 1 of chart 8-st rep a total of 3 times. Cont to foll chart through row 19, then cont in St st with MC to end of piece, AT SAME

TIME, inc 1 st each side every 6th (4th) row 6 (8) times—36 (40) sts. Work even until piece measures 9½ (12)" / 24 (30.5) cm from beg. Bind off.

finishing

Block pieces to measurements. Sew shoulder seam. Set in sleeves. Sew side and sleeve seams.

NECKBAND

With MC, pick up and k 38 (44) sts evenly around neck edge. Work in k1, p1 rib for 4 rows. Bind off.

PLACKET TRIM

With MC, pick up and k 10 sts along side of right placket. Work in k1, p1 rib for 4 rows. Bind off. Work left placket in same way, forming 2 buttonholes on row 2 by yo, k2tog at 2 sts from each end of trim. Sew on buttons.

Hat

Beg at one earflap with MC, cast on 6 sts. Working in St st, cast on 1 st at beg of every row for 10 rows—16 sts. Sl sts to a holder. Make a 2nd earflap in same way. To work the lower edge of hat with MC, cast on 10 sts, k 16 earflap sts, cast on 20 sts, k16 earflap sts, cast on 10 sts—72 sts. Work even with MC for 2 rows more.

Row 1 (WS) ★ P1 MC, p1 A; rep from ★ to end.
Row 2 (RS) ★ K1 MC, k1 A; rep from ★ to end.

CHART PAT

Next row (WS) Beg with row 5, work chart 8-st rep 9 times, until row 15 is completed. Then, work rows 2 and 1 (not 1 and 2). Work even with MC for 3 rows.

SHAPE CROWN

Row 1 (RS) [K4, k2tog] 12 times—60 sts.

Rows 2, 4, 6 and 8 Purl.
Row 3 [K3, k2tog] 12 times—48 sts.
Row 5 [K2, k2tog] 12 times—36 sts.
Row 7 [K1, k2tog] 12 times—24 sts.
Row 9 [K2tog] 12 times—12 sts. Cut yarn leaving a long end. Pull yarn through rem sts and draw up tightly to secure top of crown. Sew back seam. Block lightly. With crochet hook and A, work an edge of sc evenly around lower edge and earflaps. Join and fasten off.

fair isle chart

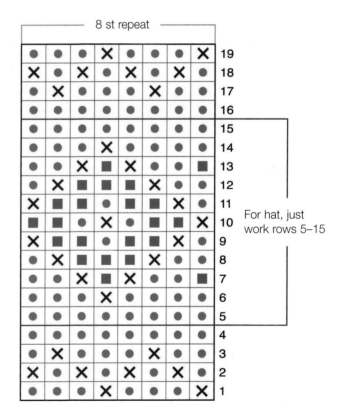

8 st repeat

For hat, just work rows 5–15

COLOR KEY

● Beige (MC)
✕ Brown (A)
■ Blue (B)

summer fun

When temperatures rise it's easy to stay cool in a crisp little sundress and matching hat, featuring a simple stockinette stitch bodice that you reverse for the skirt to add a little texture. A delicate floral ribbon and crochet trim enhance the look to make your little one feel like a princess.

SIZE

DRESS

To fit 1 (2, 3) years. Shown in size 2 years.

HAT

To fit one size, 2 years as shown.

FINISHED MEASUREMENTS

DRESS

- Chest 21 (22, 23)" / 53 (56, 58.5) cm
- Length 15¼ (16½, 18¾)" / 39 (42, 47.5) cm

HAT

- Head circumference 16" (40.5 cm)
- Depth 7" (18 cm)

MATERIALS

DRESS

 5 (5, 6) x 1 oz. (25 g) skeins, each approx. 108 yd. (99 m) long, of Tahki Stacy Charles *Cotton Classic* (cotton) in #3411 Orange

- One size 6 (4 mm) circular needle, 24" (60 cm) long OR SIZE NECESSARY TO OBTAIN CORRECT GAUGE
- Size F/5 (4 mm) crochet hook
- 1 yd. (90 cm) of floral ribbon
- Stitch marker

HAT

- 1 x 1 oz. (25 g) skein approx. 108 yd. (99 m) long, of Tahki Stacy Charles *Cotton Classic* (cotton) in #3411 Orange
- Size 6 (4 mm) needles OR SIZE NECESSARY TO OBTAIN CORRECT GAUGE
- Size F/5 (4 mm) crochet hook
- 1 yd. (90 cm) of floral ribbon

GAUGE

20 sts and 26 rows/rnds = 4" (10 cm) over St st using size 6 (4 mm) needles. BE SURE TO CHECK THE GAUGE.

Dress

body

Beg at lower edge, cast on 160 (168, 176) sts. Join being careful not to twist sts. Pm to mark beg of rnd. Working in rnds of reverse St st (p every rnd), work even until piece measures 9 (10, 11½)" / 23 (25.5, 29) cm from beg.

BODICE

Next rnd [K2, k2tog] 40 (42, 44) times—120 (126, 132) sts. K1 rnd even.

Next rnd [K6, (7, 7), k2tog] 14 times, k8 (0, 6)—106 (112, 118) sts.

Cont to work bodice even in St st for 3 (3, 3½)" / 7.5 (7.5, 9) cm more.

fashion tip Use the leftover floral ribbon to make cute friendship bracelets.

DIVIDE FOR ARMHOLES

NOTE Work back and forth in rows to the end of the piece.

Next row Bind off 4 sts, k 49 (52, 55), turn. Cont on these sts only for back of dress, work as foll:

Next row (WS) Bind off 4 sts, purl to end. Then cont in St st, dec 1 st each end of next 3 rows—39 (42, 45) sts. Work 1 row even.

SHAPE NECK

Next row (RS) K16 (17, 18) sts, join a 2nd ball of yarn and bind off center 7 (8, 9) sts, k to end. Working both sides at once, dec 1 st at each neck edge on the next 5 rows—11 (12, 13) sts rem each side, work even until armhole measures 3¼ (3½, 3¾)" / 8 (9, 9.5) cm. Bind off.

front

Rejoin yarn to the rem sts and bind off 4 sts, work to end. Cont to shape armhole binding off 4 sts at beg of next row, then dec 1 st each side on the next 3 rows—39 (42, 45) sts. Complete same as back.

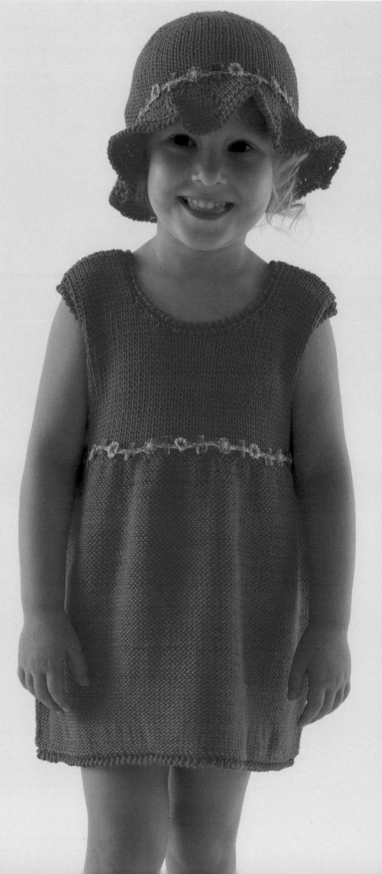

finishing

Block pieces to measurements. Sew shoulder seams. With crochet hook, work sc evenly around neck edge. Ch 1, do not turn, then working from left to right, work 1 backwards sc in each sc. Work edge in same way around the armholes and hem of dress. Sew ribbon trim onto the bodice as shown in the photo.

Hat

Beg above the brim, cast on 81 sts. Work in St st for 3" (7.5 cm).

SHAPE CROWN
Row 1 [K8, k2tog] 8 times, k1—73 sts.
Row 2 and all even rows Purl.
Row 3 [K7, k2tog] 8 times, k1—65 sts.
Row 5 [K6, k2tog] 8 times, k1—57 sts.
Row 7 [K5, k2tog] 8 times, k1—49 sts.
Row 9 [K4, k2tog] 8 times, k1—41 sts.
Row 11 [K3, k2tog] 8 times, k1—33 sts.
Row 13 [K2, k2tog] 8 times, k1—25 sts.
Row 15 [K1, k2tog] 8 times, k1—17 sts.
Row 17 [K2tog] 8 times, k1—9 sts.
Cut yarn leaving a long end. Pull through sts and draw up tightly to close top. Leave end hanging but do not sew back seam.

BRIM

From RS, pick up and k 81 sts along the cast-on edge of hat.
Row 1 (RS) P, inc 19 sts evenly spaced—100 sts.
Row 2 [K7, inc 1 st in next st] 12 times, k4—112 sts.
Rows 3, 5 and 7 Purl.
Row 4 [K8, inc 1 st in next st] 12 times, k4—124 sts.
Row 6 [K9, inc 1 st in next st] 12 times, k4—136 sts.
Row 8 [K10, inc 1 st in next st] 12 times, k4—148 sts.
Row 9 Knit.
Row 10 [K11, inc 1 st in next st] 12 times, k4—160 sts.
Bind off knitwise.

finishing

Block to measurements. Sew back seam. Working around lower brim with crochet hook, from left to right, work 1 backwards sc in each st around. Fasten off. Sew ribbon trim onto the brim as shown in the photo.

fashion tip Buy some bright orange flip-flops and glue some ribbon trim on to the thongs to match the hat—a girl needs some cute accessories!

square dance

Lively little squares dance across this sturdy and colorful pullover. The bright colors and machine-washable wool stack up to make the perfect sweater for the preschool set. Knitting this one might take a little bit of getting used to but once you master the steps you'll be moving right along.

SIZE

To fit sizes newborn–6 months (12 months, 18 months). Shown in size 12 months.

FINISHED MEASUREMENTS

- Chest 21 (24, 27)" / 53 (61, 68.5) cm
- Length 11 (12, 14)" / 28 (30.5, 35.5) cm
- Upper arm 9 (9½, 10¾)" / 23 (24, 27) cm

MATERIALS

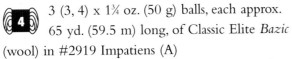

- 3 (3, 4) x 1¾ oz. (50 g) balls, each approx. 65 yd. (59.5 m) long, of Classic Elite *Bazic* (wool) in #2919 Impatiens (A)
- 2 x 1¾ oz. (50 g) balls, each approx. 65 yd. (59.5 m) long, of Classic Elite *Bazic* (wool) in #2961 Carnation (B), #2958 Barn Red (C), #2925 Sunflower (D), and #2955 Sun Opal (E)
- Size 9 (5.5 mm) needles OR SIZE NECESSARY TO OBTAIN CORRECT GAUGE
- Size 9 (5.5 mm) circular needle 16" (40 cm) long
- Bobbins (optional)
- Safety pin
- Stitch markers

GAUGE

16 sts and 18 rows = 4" (10 cm) over St st using size 9 (5.5 mm) needles. BE SURE TO CHECK THE GAUGE.

NOTE Work each block of color with a separate ball of yarn (or bobbin). Do not carry colors across back of work.

BLOCK PATTERN

The block pattern for front or back is worked over 7 (8, 9) sts for each square, and 8 (8, 10) rows long in the foll color sequence:
Row 1 of squares 7 (8, 9) sts each in B, E, D, A, C, B. Worked for 8 (8, 10) rows.
Row 2 of squares D, A, C, B, E, D.
Row 3 of squares C, B, E, D, A, C.
Row 4 of squares E, D, A, C, B, E.
Row 5 of squares A, C, B, E, D, A.
Row 6 of squares B, E, D, A, C, B.
Row 7 of squares D, A, C, B, E, D.

Sweater

back

With straight needles and A, cast on 42 (48, 54) sts. Work in k2, p2 rib for 1" (2.5 cm).

BLOCK PATTERN

Foll the instructions for block pat for chosen size, work in St st and block pat, with 8 (8, 10) rows in each row of squares, until piece measures 11 (12, 14)" / 28 (30.5, 35.5) cm from beg. Bind off.

front

Work as for back until piece measures 8 (9, 11)" / 20.5 (23, 28) cm from beg.

SEPARATE FOR V NECK

Next row (RS) Work 20 (23, 26) sts, sl next 2 sts to a safety pin for v neck, work across row to end. Working both sides at once, dec 1 st at each neck edge *every* row 6 times, then every other row twice—12 (15, 16) sts rem each side. When there are same number of rows as back, bind off sts each side for shoulders.

sleeves

With A, cast on 22 (24, 26) sts. Work in k2, p2 rib for 1" (2.5 cm), dec 1 (0, inc 1) st on last WS row—21 (24, 27) sts.

BLOCK PATTERN

Next row (RS) Beg with row 4 of squares, work in pat as for back inc 1 st each side every 4th row 7 (7, 8) times—36 (38, 43) sts. Work even until piece measures 8 (8, 9)" / 20.5 (20.5, 23) cm from beg. Bind off.

finishing

Block pieces lightly to measurements. Sew shoulder seams. Place markers at 4½ (4¾, 5½)" / 11.5 (12, 14) cm down from shoulders. Sew sleeve to armholes between markers. Sew side and sleeve seams.

NECKBAND

With circular needle and A, pick up and k 52 sts evenly around neck edge, including 2 sts on safety pin at center front. Join and pm to mark beg of rnd. Working in k2, p2 rib (with k2 rib falling at center of V neck), work in k2, p2 rib for 3 rnds, dec 1 st each side of center 2 k sts every rnd. Bind off.

pint-size **pullover** **and hat**

Chase away the chill with this pint-size snuggly pullover and matching cap. Worked effortlessly in garter stitch, this is a real beginner's project. The cap is worked in a rectangle and then gathered at the top so you don't have to do any shaping. So easy you can make one for all your favorite tots.

SIZE

To fit newborn–6 (9, 12, 18, 24) months.

FINISHED MEASUREMENTS

PULLOVER

- Chest 20 (22, 24½, 26½, 28)" / 51 (56, 62, 67, 71) cm
- Length 11 (11½, 12½, 13¼, 14)" / 28 (29, 32, 33.5, 35.5) cm
- Upper arm 8½ (9, 9¾, 10¼, 11)" / 21.5 (23, 25, 26, 28) cm

HAT

- Head circumference 13 (13 13¾, 14¼, 15, 15)" / 33 (35, 36, 38, 38) cm
- Depth 5 (5, 5½, 5½, 6)" / 12.5 (12.5, 14, 14, 15) cm

MATERIALS

 2 (2, 3, 3, 4) x 3½ oz. (100 g) balls, each approx. 220 yd. (213 m) long, of Patons *Classic Merino Wool* (wool) in #240 Leaf Green
- Size 10 (6 mm) needles OR SIZE NECESSARY TO OBTAIN CORRECT GAUGE
- Safety pin
- Stitch markers

GAUGE

14 sts and 28 rows = 4" (10 cm) over garter st using size 10 (6 mm) needles. BE SURE TO CHECK THE GAUGE.

NOTE The yarn weight is a classic worsted weight, but the gauge is a loose knit garter on a larger size needle than is customarily used for this weight. It is important to cast on and bind off loosely.

PULLOVER

back

Cast on 35 (39, 43, 47, 49) sts loosely. Work in garter st (k every row) until piece measures 11 (11½, 12½, 13¼, 14)" / 28 (29, 32, 33.5, 35.5) cm from beg. Bind off loosely.

front

Work as for back until piece measures 7½ (8, 9, 9¾, 10)" / 19 (20.5, 23, 23.5, 25.5) cm from beg.

SEPARATE FOR V NECK

Next row (RS) K 17 (19, 21, 23, 24) sts, place center st on a safety pin, join a 2nd ball of yarn and k rem 17 (19, 21, 23, 24) sts. Working both sides at once, dec 1 st at each neck edge every 2nd row 4 times, every 4th row 3 times—10 (12, 14, 16, 17) sts rem each side. Work even until there are same

number of rows as back to shoulders. Bind off sts loosely each side.

sleeves

Cast on 22 (22, 24, 24, 26) sts loosely. Work in garter st inc 1 st each side every 8th row 4 (5, 5, 6, 6) times—30 (32, 34, 36, 38) sts. Work even until piece measures 7 (7, 7, 8, 10½)" / 18 (18, 18, 20.5, 26.5) cm from beg. Bind off loosely.

finishing

Do not block. Sew left shoulder seam.

NECKBAND

Pick up and k 1 st in each st across back neck, 1 st in every ridge (or every other row) to center V neck, 1 st from safety pin, 1 st in every ridge on other side of V neck. Work in garter st for 3 rows, dec 1 st each side of center V-neck st on first and

3rd rows. Bind off. Sew other shoulder seam. Place markers at 4¼ (4½, 4¾, 5, 5½)" / 10.5 (11.5, 12.5, 13, 14) cm down from shoulders. Sew sleeves to armholes between markers. Sew side and sleeve seams.

Hat

Cast on 46 (48, 50, 52, 52) sts. Work in garter st for 8 (8, 8½, 8½, 9)" / 20.5 (20.5, 21.5, 21.5, 23) cm. Bind off.

finishing

Sew back seam of hat (the sides of the rows form the back seam) leaving a long end of yarn. Pull yarn through the bound off sts at top and draw up tightly to form the hat's crown. Make a 2½" (6.5 cm) pompom (see page 99) and attach to top of hat.

springtime patchwork

Pinks and greens evoke a lively springtime feeling in this glorious little blanket. Worked in squares it is a perfect take-along project. Once you have completed the squares they can be stitched together and then a few little posies added for good measure. Machine-washable cotton blend is ideal for the season.

FINISHED MEASUREMENTS
- Width 25" (63.5 cm) including edge
- Length 31" (78.5 cm) including edge

MATERIALS
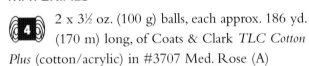
2 x 3½ oz. (100 g) balls, each approx. 186 yd. (170 m) long, of Coats & Clark *TLC Cotton Plus* (cotton/acrylic) in #3707 Med. Rose (A)
- 1 x 3½ oz. (100 g) ball approx. 186 yd. (170 m) long, of Coats & Clark *TLC Cotton Plus* (cotton/ acrylic) in #3643 Kiwi (B), #3100 Cream (C), and #3706 Lt. Rose (D)
- Size 8 (5 mm) needles OR SIZE NECESSARY TO OBTAIN CORRECT GAUGE
- Size H/8 (5 mm) crochet hook
- Tapestry needle
- Embroidery floss

GAUGE
- 16 sts and 18 rows = 4" (10 cm) over St st using size 8 (5 mm) needles.
- 20 sts and 24 rows = 4" (10 cm) over pat st using size 8 (5 mm) needles. BE SURE TO CHECK THE GAUGE.

PATTERN STITCH
Row 1 (RS) ★ K1, p1; rep from ★ to end.
Row 2 Knit.
Rep rows 1 and 2 for pat st.

Blanket

stockinette stitch squares
Make 2 each in colors A and B, 1 each in colors C and D, for a total of 6 squares. Cast on 26 sts. Work in St st for 6" (15 cm). Bind off.

pattern stitch squares
Make 3 each in colors A and B, 4 each in colors C and D. Cast on 30 sts. Work in pat st for 6" (15 cm). Bind off.

finishing
Block lightly. Using template opposite and photo as a guide, with tapestry needle, embroider flowers on 4 of the St st squares in contrast yarn colors. Sew squares tog, 4 squares across and 5 down (or as desired).

CROCHET EDGE
With crochet hook and A, join with Sl st in one corner and work 20 sc in a side of each square, with 3 sc in each corner. Join and ch 1.
Next rnd ★ Work 1 sc, skip 2 sc, 5 dc in next st, skip 2 sts; rep from ★ around. Join and fasten off.

embroidery tip Use floss colors that will provide contrast with the individual square you are embellishing.

embroidery template

how to get started

This section includes all the basic techniques you will need to get started, from casting on for the first time, to shaping, and binding off your work. If you are coming to knitting for the first time, read through all the techniques carefully, and practice any tricky bits until you are confident enough to try one of the easier patterns.

Maintaining gauge

holding the needles

The position of the needles is also crucial to the finished gauge of your knitting. Some knitters hold both needles evenly in front of them, while others secure one needle under the right arm and let the left needle drop diagonally. Yet another style is to secure both needles, one under each arm. It does not matter which style you choose, as long as you feel comfortable, without any strain on your hands, back, or neck, and can work easily.

Hold the needles evenly in front of the body, with the hands taking equal weight. This method is favored by beginners knitting for the first time.

Here the right-hand needle is held firmly under the arm, leaving the right hand free to tension the yarn. The weight of the knitting is held under your arm.

holding the yarn

Holding the yarn will come with practice and may feel awkward at the start. Everyone finds a way to tension the yarn so that it flows evenly through the fingers. These instructions are for a right-handed knitter.

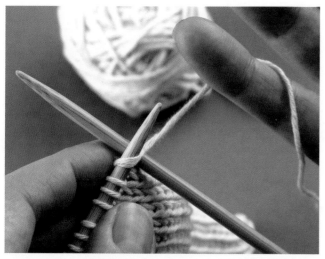

1 Hold the needles in your left hand. With your right palm upper-most, take the yarn round your little finger.

2 As you turn your right hand over, wrap the yarn over your ring finger and under your middle finger.

3 Your index finger will control the yarn; hold your hand so that this finger can easily loop over the needles. To maintain tension, readjust this movement from time to time.

reading the label All knitting yarns will have a number or date on the ball band, or inside the cone, that relates to the batch in which it was dyed. It is essential to check this number when purchasing yarn, making sure that all your balls are from the same batch. Although it may not be obvious at this stage, any yarn from a different dye vat will definitely stand out when the garment is finished.

Making a slipknot
This is the essential first step in knitting. Making a slipknot will allow you to begin casting on for a new project.

1 Make a loop by passing the right side of the yarn over the left.

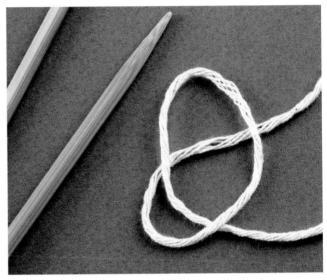

2 Pass the tail end under the loop. Now pass it through the first loop.

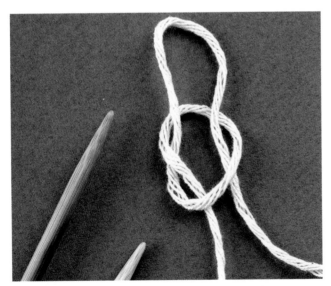

3 Pull the tail end to secure the slipknot.

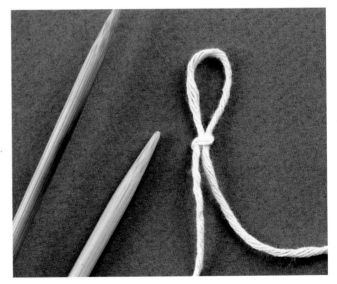

4 Adjust the loop to the correct size for your thumb or knitting needle, depending on which cast-on method you use.

Casting on This is the first row of your knitting and usually creates the bottom edge of your work. Find a way that works for you and your project.

long end casting on

This is also known as the "thumb" method. To calculate the amount of yarn needed for the long end, estimate the finished length of the cast-on edge, and multiply by three.

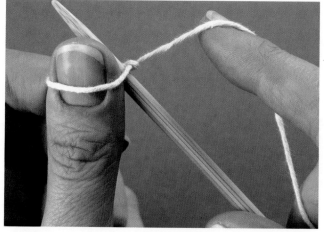

1 Make a slipknot with your yarn, leaving a tail that is long enough to cast on the number of stitches required. Place the loop on your thumb, and insert the point from the right needle into the loop.

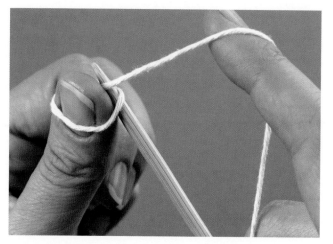

2 With your right hand, wrap the yarn around the point of the needle and between the needle and your thumb.

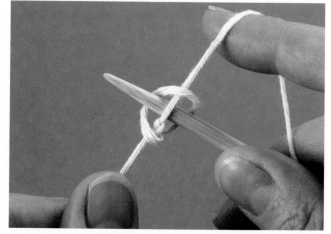

3 Draw through the loop on the thumb, then slip the loop over the edge of the needle, knit the loop and make a stitch.

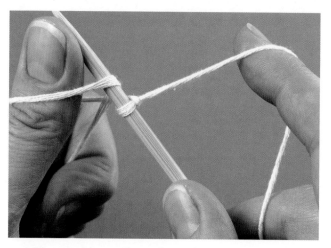

4 Keep going until you have the required number of stitches on the needle.

casting on with two needles

This method works only if the first row of knitting will be worked into the back of the stitches in the casting-on row. If you do not do this, the edge of your work will be loopy.

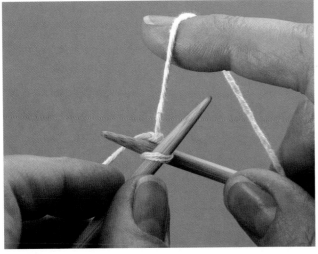

1 Make a slipknot and put it onto the left needle. Put the right needle into the loop so that it passes under the left.

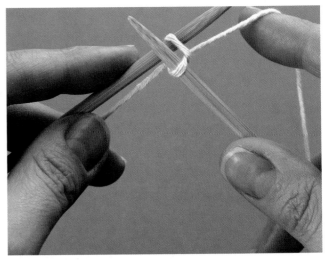

2 Pass the yarn between the needles and take the yarn through the first loop with the right needle.

3 Then pass the second loop from the right needle to the left.

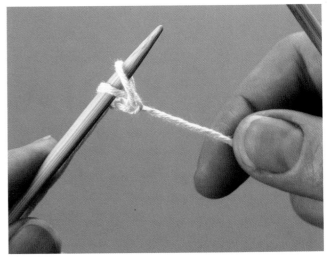

4 Repeat by putting the right needle into the last stitch on the left needle until you have made the required number of stitches.

cable casting on

This method makes a strong edge and is more decorative than the other casting-on methods, though it may not be as elastic. Follow the method for casting on with two needles for the first two stitches, then make the remaining stitches as follows.

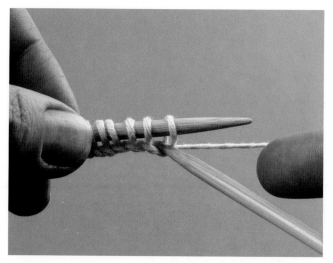

1 Place the right needle between the first and second stitches.

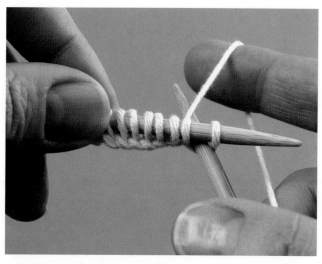

2 Pass the yarn around the back and between the two needles.

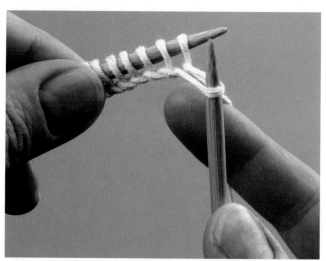

3 Pull the loop on the right hand needle towards you. Pass the yarn around the back and between the two needles.

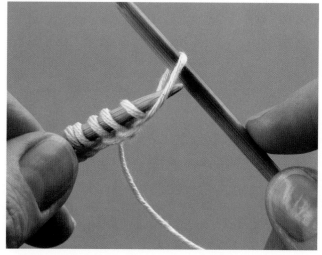

4 Place this new stitch with the other stitches on the left needle. Repeat until the required number of stitches is made.

Basic stitches
All knitted fabrics are made up of one or two stitches—knit and purl. Working a knit row and then a purl row alternately produces stockinette stitch, which is used in most simple patterns. With stockinette stitch, the knit side is the right side.

knit stitch
This is the basic knitting stitch. If you only made knit stitches you would end up with garter stitch.

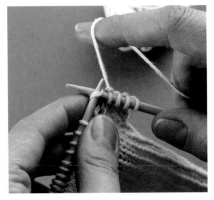

1 Cast on the required stitches onto the left needle. Insert the point of the right needle from front to back through the first loop on the left needle.

2 Pass the yarn (which is always at the back of work for plain knitting) between the two needle points, as shown.

3 Draw the loop through to the front of the work. Pull the left needle under the right one, drawing the loop through with it.

4 Slip the remaining stitch off the left needle. Your stitch will now be on the right needle. Continue like this to the end of the row.

5 To knit the next row, turn your work around so the back is facing you and the stitches are on your left needle again. The empty right needle is ready to receive the next row of stitches.

purl stitch

This is identical to the knit stitch, but is just done backwards. If you knitted all purl stitches, you would have garter stitch, just as if you had worked only knit stitches.

1 Beginning with the yarn at the front insert the right needle from back to front into the first stitch on the left needle.

2 Pass the yarn (which for purl is always held in front of your work) over and around the point of the right needle.

3 Draw the loop through.

4 Slide the first stitch off the left needle. Continue like this to the end of the row.

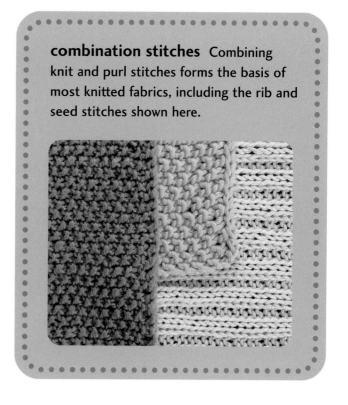

combination stitches Combining knit and purl stitches forms the basis of most knitted fabrics, including the rib and seed stitches shown here.

Shaping
Increasing or decreasing the number of stitches is how knitwear is shaped. Once you have mastered the art of shaping, you can knit any kind of garment or shape.

increasing
This can be done anywhere in a row, but it should always be done where specified in the pattern.

KNITTING INTO THE BACK OF A STITCH
This is where the increase is made on the first or last stitch in a row, and it creates one extra stitch at the increase point. Knit the first stitch, but instead of dropping the stitch off the left needle, place the point of the right needle into the back of the stitch, knit it and then drop it off the left needle. You now have two stitches on the right needle. Work purl increases in the same way, but purlwise.

FULLY FASHIONED INCREASING
This is where the increase is made not on the first or last stitch but usually on the third stitch from the edge. It may also be made on the second stitch from the edge or across the work at regular points, if you want to widen your work suddenly as a feature.

The mark made when increasing in this way is called a fashioning mark, and this technique is often used as a design feature, particularly on finer knitwear or when using a smooth yarn such as mercerized cotton. This visible mark on your work is also useful for counting your increases.

1 On a knit row, knit the first two stitches.

2 Then knit the third stitch, but instead of dropping this stitch off the left needle, place the point of the right needle into the back of the stitch, knit this loop too, then drop the stitch off the needle.

decreasing

This is the shaping that makes your work narrower. You do this by knitting or purling two stitches together to reduce them to one stitch.

SIMPLE DECREASING

Pass the tip of the right needle through the first two stitches on the left needle and work together, producing one stitch on the right needle. For purl rows, work as above but decrease purlwise.

FULLY FASHIONED DECREASING

This works two stitches together, but instead of knitting together the end two stitches, work together the second and third or third and fourth stitches to produce a fashioning mark on the right side of your work. This method will produce a slope from left to right. For purl rows, work as above but purlwise.

Sometimes a pattern uses decreases on both sides of a garment, and uses the marks as a design feature, then it is important that the stitches slope in the correct way.

To get a right-to-left slope on a knit row, at the decrease point, slip the first stitch (pass it to the other needle without knitting it), knit the next stitch, then pass the slipped stitch over the knitted stitch. To get a right-to-left slope on a purl row, purl the first stitch and then put it back onto the left needle, lift the next stitch over it, and then return it to the right needle.

Binding off
Always bind off in the appropriate stitch for your work—that is knitwise on a knit row and purlwise on a purl row. Binding off on a purl row will have less of a tendency to roll, and the edge is less visible from the right side. If binding off a rib, bind off in both knit and purl, following the rib pattern.

simple binding off
On a purl row, purl the first two stitches then bind off as described below, but purling every stitch. It is not necessary to bind off between every stitch. On a knit row, work as follows.

1 On a knit row, knit the first two stitches.

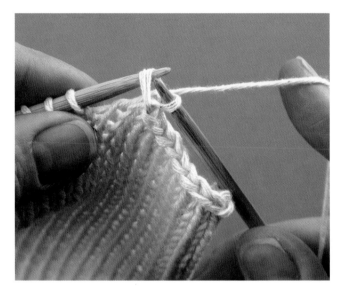

2 With the left needle, lift the first stitch over the second, then knit the second stitch (which is now the first on the needle). Follow this pattern of lifting one stitch over the next then knitting the next stitch until just one stitch remains. Break off the yarn and pass the tail through the last loop.

binding off When binding off for children's clothes it is sometimes best to bind off with needles two sizes bigger than the ones you used for knitting the rest of the garment. Another way of avoiding a tight bind-off edge is to pick up, knit, then bind off the loop lying between each of the stitches on the needle.

Repairing a dropped stitch
Try to repair a dropped stitch and correct your work from the right side. To repair a dropped stitch on the wrong side of your work, repair in the same way but with your stitch at the back of your work. If you are repairing a stitch in a patterned piece of work, make sure you knit or purl where appropriate.

1 Make sure that your stitch is at the front of your work and then use your knitting needle or a crochet hook to pick up the horizontal threads, pulling each thread through the stitch one at a time until you have picked up all the dropped stitches.

2 Place the stitch back on your needle.

Using a stitch marker
A useful knitter's tool required in many of the patterns.

Wrap a contrast-colored piece of yarn around the stitch you wish to mark and tie it in a double knot.

Alternatively, use plastic markers sold in notions departments or yarn stores.

using color

There are two main ways of incorporating color into your work. Fair Isle is a traditional method where two colors in each row build up a complicated-looking pattern. Intarsia is used to make larger motifs or blocks of color. Difficulties with both techniques are keeping the tension smooth, and managing those extra balls of yarn.

Intarsia

You can work intarsia in both knit and purl. At the appropriate point, add a second color by twisting the two yarns around each other on the wrong side where they meet, so avoiding gaps in the work. Repeat this process on each row where colors meet.

1 This is what the join will look like on the reverse of your work. Note that the two colors are linked together at the join to prevent gaps appearing.

2 On the right side there should be no holes or changes in gauge if the yarn is linked evenly behind.

3 Here you can see the yarn twisting together where the colors join. It is important to keep the tension even to avoid puckering at this point. When the work is finished, you will need to weave the ends vertically down the loops where the colors meet. Never weave the ends horizontally into the work, as this will show on the right side and may also unravel, appearing on the right side.

Fair Isle When knitting Fair Isle, you will usually have two colors on each row, and the colors not being used must be woven or stranded across the back of the work. There are two main techniques used for this: stranding and weaving in.

STRANDING

Stranding is where the yarn is left loose across the back of the work, but will never pass more than four or five stitches before being picked up and used again. Stranding is the traditional method used in the Shetland Islands, and is often preferred to weaving in because it keeps a softer, more pliable feel to the work. However, if these strands are pulled too tightly across the back of the work they can greatly distort the work and result in an uneven fabric.

WEAVING IN

Weaving in, by contrast, is where the yarn not being knitted is woven over and under the color in use. The color not in use is passed over the color in use when knitting one stitch, and under the color in use on the following stitch. This creates a thicker fabric without the floating threads at the back of the work. Anyone who has dressed a baby will know that any threads that are not sewn in will get caught on tiny fingers and toes, and so weaving in may be preferable here.

The back of the work here shows stranding across several stitches.

The pattern at the front of the work should be even and flat. If the threads are pulled unevenly at the back of the work it will gather the fabric.

To weave in, twist the threads together at the back of each stitch so as not to leave long running threads.

using up yarn Knitting for babies and children is a great way to use up all those small oddments of yarn that you didn't know what to do with. Projects should be completed quickly, which is good for a novice knitter, or someone who doesn't have much spare knitting time.

Managing color

When working in intarsia or Fair Isle you will need small amounts of the contrast colors. If you are using lots of colors in a row it can be useful to have a small wrapping or bobbin of each separate color. Try to keep each color in its own small bag, or even a jam jar, to prevent the balls from getting tangled together and unraveling out of control. Use one of the following methods to make a separate wrapping of each yarn color.

WINDING BY HAND

Using your the thumb and little finger, wrap the yarn in a figure of eight to the required amount. Break off from the main ball, and then secure the end around the center of the bundle. This method should keep the wrap in shape and avoid tangling.

PLASTIC BOBBINS

You can also buy plastic bobbins that can make the process easier.

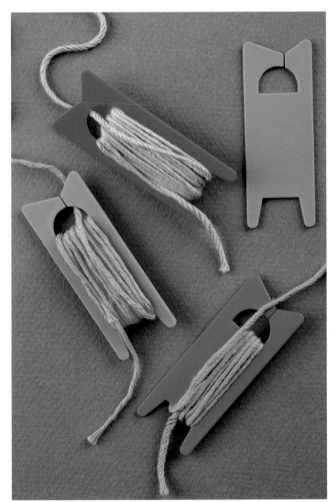

SKEINS

Occasionally yarn still comes on skeins, especially from small specialist manufacturers. There is a tool available called a knitter's umbrella, or "niddy noddy," that unfolds allowing you to place the skein onto it, this will then turn as you wind off your yarn into a ball. However they seem to be harder to come by these days so you may have to use another pair of hands or the back of a chair to hold the skein while you wind.

A ball winder is also available in some specialist shops, which enables you to wind a ball in the shape of a squat cylinder. When removed from the winder you can take the yarn from the center of the ball, which will avoid your ball traveling all around the floor as you knit.

However enthusiastic you may be about starting a pattern, always spend time organising your yarn first.

joining in a new color Always tie the ends together when joining a new color or fresh ball of yarn to your work. This will prevent a hole appearing due to unraveling ends. As you add a new color or fresh yarn, always leave long ends—they are useful for sewing up the seams of your work.

finishing your work

This section contains a variety of finishing techniques, including adding buttonholes and making a pom-pom. You will also find a variety of embroidery stitches to embellish your work, and some reliable methods to join pieces of work together.

Buttonholes It is important to correctly position buttonholes—two or three stitches in from the edge of the work—because they create a gauge in your work. It is worth over-sewing your buttonhole to give it a firm edge, since with time wear on the threads on either side of the hole may cause the yarn to break and unravel. Simply work an overstitch or small blanket stitch around each buttonhole to protect the edge.

horizontal

This is the most common buttonhole to work. It is used where the strain on the buttonhole is from side to side.

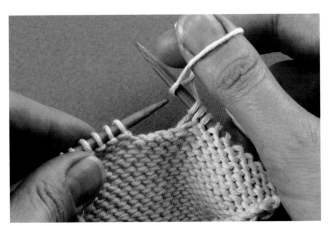

1 At the required position, and starting on a knit row, bind off the number of stitches required for the size of your button. On the return row, cast on over the bound-off stitches using the thumb method (see page 79), and work to the end of the row.

2 On the following rows, knit or purl the stitches according to your pattern, so that the number of stitches in the row is restored.

vertical

Use this style where the strain on the button is up or down. Divide your work in two to make a vertical slit. Where the buttonhole begins, keep the remaining stitches on a stitch holder and continue knitting the stitches on your needle until the buttonhole measures the required length. Place these stitches on a stitch holder. Repeat the process on the opposite side. When the work is of the same length, continue on all the stitches together, so completing the buttonhole.

sewing on a button correctly

Where possible, use strands of yarn from your work to attach the button firmly. Create a shank by wrapping the yarn around the base of the button to strengthen the threads that join the button to the garment.

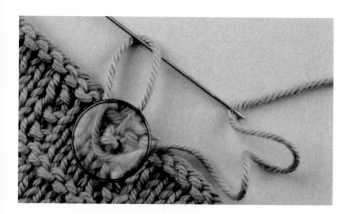

eyelet

This buttonhole is suitable for fine knitwear or baby wear and can also be used as a method for threading ribbon around the edges of a knitted garment.

1 Working on a knit row, when you come to the place to make the eyelet buttonhole, put the yarn forward, as shown.

2 Knit the next two stitches together. In the next row, the made stitch is purled in the usual way.

Cables

A cable pattern, which is usually worked on the knit row, gives an embossed effect to your knitting. There are numerous variations on cable patterns, some of which look very complicated but are worth attempting for their stunning results.

In addition to your yarn and knitting needles, you will need a cable needle (cn) or double-pointed needle (dpn) to work a cable. The cn holds the stitches so that the twist in your work can be made. Slip the first group of stitches in your cable onto the cn, then place this either at the front or back of your work (see below). Knit the number of stitches specified in the pattern, followed by the stitches from the cn.

Holding the stitches on the cn at the back of your work produces a cable that twists to the right, while holding the stitches on the cn at the front of your

work gives a cable that twists to the left. If you are knitting two cables on either side of a textured panel, making one cable twist to the right and the other to the left will give your work a pleasing symmetry.

Most basic cables are crossed after you have worked the same number of rows as there are stitches in the cable width. By crossing the stitches after fewer rows have been worked, a more corded effect is achieved. To cross a basic four-stitch cable, work as follows.

1 Follow your pattern to the cable cross row, then work to the four stitches of the cable. There will usually be at least one purl stitch on either side of a cable, which helps the cable stand out. Put the next two stitches onto the cn.

2 Knit the next two stitches, then knit the two stitches from the cn.

3 Continue working in the pattern to the end.

Pockets

There are two types of pocket you could add to your knitted work: concealed pockets and patch pockets. Patch pockets are a simpler technique, preferred by beginners.

concealed pocket

1 Make a pocket bag by knitting in stockinette stitch to the width and length required, keeping the stitches on a stitch holder. Then work the garment until you reach the row that corresponds with the top of the pocket.

2 Work the pattern to where the edge of the pocket will begin, then slip the same number of stitches as there are on the pocket top onto a separate stitch holder. Continue in pattern across the stitches from the pocket lining, and then continue across the remaining stitches of the main work to the end of the row.

3 (top right) When the work is complete, pick up the stitches from the stitch holder, and work in rib or whatever pattern is required for finishing the pocket top.

4 (right) Sew the pocket bag to the inside of the garment along the two sides and bottom, always trying to follow a vertical line of stitches on the side seams to assure a straight pocket.

patch pocket

1 Make a pocket by knitting a square in the stitch required for your pattern (usually stockinette stitch) and to the correct size, usually finishing with a rib.

2 When the pocket bag is finished, attach it to the front of your work around three sides, following the lines of the knitting to assure a straight pocket. Alternatively, you can attach the cast-on edge to your work when you reach the row where the base of the pocket will start, by working together the stitches from the main body with the cast-on edge of the pocket bag.

Picot hem
This creates a pretty scallopped edge on cuffs, hems, and edges. This is a classic technique for adding pretty details to children's clothes.

1 Cast on an odd number of stitches. Work in stockinette stitch for the depth of the hem edge, ending on a purl row. On the next row, make a row of holes by working k1, yfd, k2tog, to the end of the row. Work in stockinette stitch for the same number of rows from the cast-on edge to the row of holes.

2 Turn up the hem and sew it with a catch stitch. Pick up one stitch from either side of the work, where the cast-on edge meets the row of knitted fabric. The stitch is worked diagonally with a darning needle and thread. Alternatively, knit up the hem by knitting together one stitch from the needle with one loop from the cast-on edge, by putting the loop from the cast-on edge onto the left needle and knitting it together with the next stitch.

Making a tie cord
This simple technique can include more than one color of yarn to make a jazzy, multicolored cord that will complement the finished knitwear.

1 Cut yarn eight times as long as the cord length required. Fold in half, then in half again (four ends together). Hold firmly at one end then twist the other end very tightly in a clockwise direction.

2 Fold it in half again, and the cord will twist together. Tie a knot at one end. The tighter you twist the yarn, the better the cord will be.

Making a pom-pom
Pom-poms are fun to make, and provide great embellishments for your knitting—try using different fibers for added texture and sparkle.

1 Cut two circles of card to whatever diameter of pom-pom you require, and cut a circular hole in the center approximately 1¼" (3 cm) in diameter (or smaller for finer yarn). Alternatively, you can use a readymade pom-pom maker, as shown.

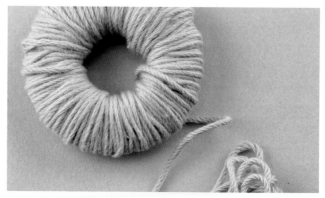

2 Put the two pieces of card together and wrap the yarn around them, threading it through the hole in the center. Cover the whole shape with yarn. The more yarn you use and the closer together you wrap the yarn, the fuller your pom-pom will be.

3 With a sharp pair of scissors, cut the threads all around the circle on the outside edge between the two pieces of card.

wrapping tip To pass yarn through the doughnut shape, wrap the yarn around a small piece of card. Pass this through the hole, unraveling the yarn as you go.

4 Ease the pieces of card apart so that you can reach the center. Wrap a piece of yarn around the center, and tie it in a tight and secure knot. Leave long ends on the knot, and use these to attach the pom-pom to your main work. Cut away and remove the card. Fluff up the pom-pom, trimming the ends if necessary for a neat finish.

Embroidery
As you become more confident, you may wish to personalize your work. Use these stitches to embellish areas of your work once the garment is finished.

chain stitch

Draw a needle through the fabric from back to front, then reinsert the needle just to the right of where it came through, holding some of the thread down to create a small loop. Take a stitch of the required length, making sure the needle passes up through the loop to form the first "chain" link. Repeat, shaping the chain stitches around your work as required. You could use this stitch as an alternative way to work the flower stems on the Springtime Patchwork blanket, featured on page 72.

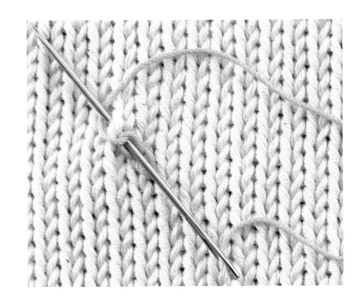

blanket stitch

1 Working from left to right, bring a darning needle, or blunt ended knitter's needle, threaded with yarn through the knitting where you want the top of the stitch to be.

2 Hold the thread down, and insert the needle to the right. Pass the needle through the loop, as shown. Pull the needle through until the thread forms a horizontal bar, and continue working to the right.

Preparation for sewing up

Different weights of garment will require different treatments before being sewn up. Generally, the heavier the fabric, the less need there is for pulling the individual pieces into place using blocking or steaming before sewing up.

blocking

This simply means pinning out the knitted pieces on a flat surface (usually a blanket or towel covered in cotton) and making sure the measurements are correct. It also enables you to pull all the stitches into place, if needed.

Pin all around the work, sticking the pins in vertically through the garment at ¾" (2 cm) intervals into the soft surface below. Do not block any ribbing that is on a garment: this should be left loose.

> **stopping knitting** Always work to the end of a row before you stop knitting. If you finish in the middle of a row, you may well find that a loop appears when you continue, because the work has stretched. In addition, you may lose your place in the row, and this will muddle the pattern you are following.

steaming

Never iron directly on your work, as it may burn or distort it, and it is hard to get a garment back to the correct shape once it has been damaged. As an alternative to pressing pieces before sewing them up, you can sew them up first and then steam the garment with strong gusts of steam from an iron.

Using a damp cloth with a hot, dry iron instead of using a steam iron is also very effective, but you must keep the cloth damp at all times. Have a bowl of water beside you as you iron, so that you can dip the cloth into it to redampen it. Place the damp cloth onto the garment and press with the hot iron.

Joining seams
Having checked your pieces and prepared them (if necessary), you are now ready for the final stages of tidying up any ends and sewing the seams. If you have used contrast colors and the yarn has met midrow, weave the ends along the meeting point of the two colors. Never sew in ends across your work, as they will show and tend to pop through to the right side.

mattress stitch
The best way to sew side seams together is using mattress stitch. It creates a wonderful flat seam that is strong and versatile and quick to do; and, if done well, it should be invisible.

1 Arrange the two pieces to be joined side by side, with their right sides facing you. Insert a threaded darning needle into the edge of one of the pieces from front to back, following a vertical line between the end and second to end stitch. Bring the needle up after two rows then pass the needle to the opposite side and repeat.

2 Continue in this way, pulling the edges together and being careful to follow the same vertical line.

finishing tip Weave in loose ends—do not leave yarn dangling inside garment.

backstitch

Use backstitch for the shoulder seams. This is a quick and firm stitch, which most people know how to do. It is done with right sides together.

edge-to-edge stitch

There is also an edge-to-edge method that will form an almost invisible seam and will avoid any bulk or hardness at shoulder seam-type edges. With right sides facing you, insert a threaded darning needle from below into the end stitch. Pull the thread through then insert the needle into the matching stitch on the opposite piece and pass through two loops, coming out onto the right side. Insert the needle back into the original stitch where the thread first appeared. This has the effect of a stitch that is sewn, not knitted.

joining work with a crochet hook

Once you have mastered crochet, this is a quick and neat way to join particularly long seams. Using a small hook, the same size of the knitting needles used or smaller, run a slipstitch along the selvage edge, picking up the loose threads between the stitches.

Once the seams have been sewn, sew in any loose yarn ends by weaving them vertically into the seams. This can also be done with a crochet hook.

caring for your knitwear

Having spent so much time making your precious garment, it is important to look after it. Knitwear for children will need to survive frequent washing. Cotton is a good choice as it is machine-washable and not scratchy next to the skin. Wool is always the warmest choice, though yarns blended with manmade fibers may be easier to care for.

washing knitwear

Always check the washing instructions on the ball band and follow them carefully. Most washing machines have special cycles for woolens and delicates that protect fibers from being weakened by too much friction and heat. As a result of this, not too much hand washing is needed any more, although you may prefer this method, certainly for any knitted lace or fine mohair. Even when using the machine, use a soap powder or liquid that is recommended for machine-washing woolens or delicates.

hand washing

It is always best to hand wash knitwear if you have lost the washing instructions for the wool used. When hand washing, use wool wash specially made for the purpose, and cool or lukewarm water. Agitate the water to make sure all the powder is dissolved, and place your knitwear in the bowl. Move it around in the water, squeezing the garment gently to allow the soapy water to permeate. Try not to rub the fibers—it is the friction that causes pilling and felting. Rinse in clean cold water until the water runs clear.

testing for color fastness

It is always advisable to wash similar colors together. Most yarns will be colorfast, but if you are not sure, dip a small piece into soapy water and press it on a white cloth. If it leaves a stain, wash it in cold water on its own. Color can transfer even in the spinning and drying process, so make sure it stays separate.

drying

Dry all knitted items, whether washed by hand or machine, flat on either a towel or clothes airer laid out horizontally, away from direct heat. Hanging knitted items on a washing line is asking for trouble. Wet sleeves will be weighed down and stretch beyond all recognition.

You can remove excess water without wringing by squeezing the knitwear gently, and using the short spin cycle on your washing machine. If the item is likely to shed significant amounts of fluff, place it inside a pillowcase or mesh washing bag to avoid clogging the machine. If you don't have a spin-dryer, or the item is particularly delicate, then roll it up in a towel and press until the worst of the water is absorbed. Next, lay the damp knitting flat on a bath towel, either on the floor, or raised off the ground on a special drying rack, and reshape with your hands. If after all this care your garment has been distorted, try steaming it back into shape under a damp kitchen towel.

felting

Felted knitting was probably introduced from the Basque region of France. This process of soaking and pummeling knitted woolen fabric was used to make the French beret. In England, knitters' apprentices used to wear elaborate felted hats.

Most of a knitter's time is spent in ensuring that their favorite knitwear does not felt during the washing process. However, felting is a marvelous way to vary the texture of a fabric and to make a garment denser and more durable.

knitting gifts If you are giving knitwear as a gift, pass on the washing instructions from the yarn label to the parent, so that they won't ruin all your hard work at the first wash. Also think about the age of the child and the season. They will only be a certain size for one season, or even less, so try and leave some growing room.

The best way to felt is to use your washing machine. Agitation is the key, so avoid the special delicate and wool cycles, as these deliberately reduce that aspect of the process. If you are concerned about clogging up the filter, place your knitting inside a pillowcase or duvet cover inside the machine.

Trial, without too much error hopefully, is key. If the knitting is not felted sufficiently, then keep washing. Don't forget that you should let the item you are felting dry out between each wash, otherwise you won't be able to tell how much it has shrunk.

storing your knitwear

It may look lovely in a magazines or fashion store, but knitted garments should never be hung on a line or hanger. Always store your knitwear neatly folded and as flat as possible.

DEALING WITH MOTHS

Moth larvae love to eat wools and natural fibers, especially if they are not completely clean. Always launder and dry knitwear thoroughly before storing for any length of time. Most infestations occur where woolens have been left undisturbed for some time in a dark place.

If you find that you have a moth problem it is best to deal with it straightaway. If infected items are recoverable, they should be sealed in a plastic bag and placed in the freezer for three days to kill off any larvae or eggs. Wash the knitwear thoroughly and air in sunlight, as moths prefer the dark. Clean out all storage chests and wardrobes with a vacuum cleaner and then keep knitwear in sealed bags with cedar wood or lavender pouches inside. Dry cleaning and ironing garments is also reputed to deter moths.

Washing symbols

These are some of the most common symbols that you will see on the ball band of your yarn. If no wash symbols are given, always assume that it is hand wash only and must be dried flat.

Symbol	Written Instruction	Meaning
[tub with 95]	Machine Wash Normal	Wash in the hottest water with detergent or soap—the yarn will withstand agitation
[tub with 60]	Machine Wash Hot	Water temperature should not exceed 65–85°F (30°C)
[tub with 40]	Machine Wash Warm	Water temperature should not exceed 105°F (40°C)
[tub with hand]	Hand Wash Only	Gentle manipulation only—in water and detergent or soap
[tub with 40 and bar]	Wool Wash	If machine-washing, you may only use the wool wash cycle
[circle in square]	Tumble Dry	A machine dryer may be used regularly at the hottest available temperature
[crossed square]	Do Not Tumble Dry	A machine dryer cannot be used
[circle with dot in square]	Tumble Dry Low	A machine dryer may be used at a low heat setting
[iron with dot]	Iron, Low	Steam or dry iron can be used regularly—temperature must not exceed 230°F (110°C)
[crossed triangle]	Do Not Bleach	Do not use chlorine bleach with this yarn
[circle]	Dry-clean	Item should be professionally dry-cleaned. It can be dry-cleaned in any solvent, cycle, moisture, or heat
[crossed circle]	Do not dry-clean	Item cannot be commercially dry-cleaned. Try airing the item in place of washing

following a pattern

Before you embark on any project it is best to read through the materials and instructions completely, so you don't end up getting stuck halfway through the project having run out of yarn, or having come across a technique or stitch you are not sure about. If you have not used a stitch before, work a swatch in the new stitch to check for mistakes. At this stage you should also familiarize yourself with any new terms or abbreviations used in the pattern or stitch glossary.

At the start of each pattern you will find a list of the equipment and materials you need to complete the pattern, including the all-important details about the gauge of the piece, the size the pattern is shown in, and the finished measurements. Where a number of different sizes are listed, work through the pattern and highlight the instructions for the particular size you are working to. The patterns in this book are also graded as to their difficulty in three categories: Easy, Intermediate, and Advanced.

yarn

The symbol by the side of the materials list with each pattern will tell you the required thickness or ply of the yarn. The pattern will indicate a make and specific color of yarn too, but with experience you will be able to substitute another yarn. As long as the new yarn is of the same ply, and your gauge matches the pattern, you should get the same results. This gives you a wider choice of yarns to work with.

This book uses the symbols from the Craft Yarn Council of America, which are intended to help standardize the way fibers are categorized. There are six groups of yarn numbered from one to six, Superfine to Super bulky. You should be able to see

changing yarn Toward the end of a ball of yarn, try to anticipate whether it will complete a row. You can estimate the length needed by multiplying the length of the row by three. If there isn't enough yarn left to complete a row, leave the end and begin a new row with a new ball. If you are really short of yarn, knit one strand of the old, and one of the new together for two stitches and weave in the ends with a tapestry needle later.

the same symbol on the ball band, making substituting yarns even easier (see symbol chart on page 110). Once you have acquired a stash of yarn you will need to organize your storage. As with finished garments, it is best to keep unused yarn in plastic bags with some moth deterrent like lavender or cedar wood.

needles

The size of needles you will need should be stated at the beginning of the pattern. Often two sizes will be indicated, one for the ribbing or neckline, and another for the main body. If you use different sizes to maintain the correct gauge, then be sure to make a note on the pattern, and change the other needles accordingly. If you start knitting with metal needles, you should continue this way, as needles made from other materials, such as wood, will affect the gauge.

gauge

The combination of yarn and needles will generally give you the gauge used in the pattern. If your gauge does not match, then change your needles and rework your sample with different needles until it does. If you have too many stitches to your 4" (10 cm) swatch, try larger needles. Conversely, if you have too few, try smaller needles.

Patterns give the expected finished measurements of your work, most importantly the width and length. You will only achieve these measurements if your gauge is correct and consistent throughout, which may take practice if you are a first time knitter.

color coding

If your pattern involves more than one color (such as in stripes or Fair Isle patterns), the pattern will provide you with the code for each color, using a system of letters to represent the different yarns and colors being used. If your pattern uses lots of colors, write the code on the ball band of each color to save confusion, or tape a some yarn onto the page as a key.

counting stitches Have a pencil and paper nearby for making notes. You will find that you often need to count your stitches to check where you are in your work. A calculator can also be handy for working out gauge or size changes.

order of work

Most garment patterns start by knitting the back, and it is advisable to work in the order set out. If you are a first time knitter, chose one of the Easy projects, which will give you the confidence to move onto the more advanced patterns.

marking progress on graphs

When following a graph, it is a good idea to use a ruler as a marker to guide your progress on each row, moving it up the graph as you complete each row, or marking each finished row with a pencil. Quite often on a complicated image no two rows are the same, so it is important to keep track of exactly where you are in the pattern.

understanding abbreviations

At their simplest, the abbreviations used on knitting patterns and in knitting books are shortened words or letters acting as shorthand for simple instructions, such as "rep" (repeat) and "k1" (knit one stitch). More complicated abbreviations, such as "psso" (pass slipped stitch over) will explain how to perform knitting methods. Most of these will be explained in the list of abbreviations (see page 111), but any special abbreviations specific to your pattern will be described in the stitch glossary at the start of the pattern.

Useful information

Wouldn't it be great if everyone used the same terms to write about yarns and needles? Unfortunately, sizes are often based on metric or imperial measurements, or are based on arbitrary systems of numbers and letters. If in doubt, use a needle gauge to find the millimeter measurement.

On these pages you will find some conversion charts that will help you to convert needles and yarns into the standard sizes that are used in the patterns.

These charts are based on the recommendations of the Craft Yarn Council of America. You can see further information on their website, www.yarnstandards.com.

yarn weights

If you are going to use a different fiber than the one recommended, it is crucial that you do a gauge swatch to ensure that you can match the gauge given at the beginning of each pattern, otherwise your knitwear will not match the finished measurements supplied.

Use the chart below as a guide to help find the right gauge for your new wool, and to choose which weight of yarn to buy to match the symbol given with each pattern.

YARN WEIGHT SYMBOL GIVEN IN THE PATTERN	1	2	3	4	5	6
TYPES OF YARNS IN CATEGORY	Sock, fingering, baby	Sport, baby	Double knitting, light worsted	Worsted, afghan, Aran	Chunky, craft, rug	Bulky, roving
KNIT GAUGE RANGE IN STOCKINETTE STITCH TO 4" (10 CM)	27–32 sts	23–26 sts	21–24sts	16–20 sts	12–15 sts	6–11 sts
RECOMMENDED NEEDLE SIZE IN METRIC RANGE	2.25–3.25 mm	3.25–4.5 mm	3.75–4.5 mm	4.5–5.5 mm	5.5–8 mm	8 mm and larger
RECOMMENDED NEEDLE SIZE	1 to 3	3 to 5	5 to 7	7 to 9	9 to 11	11 and larger
CROCHET GAUGE IN SINGLE CROCHET TO 4" (10 CM)	21–32 sts	16–20 sts	12–17 sts	11–14 sts	8–11 sts	5–9 sts
RECOMMENDED HOOK IN METRIC RANGE	2.25–3.5 mm	3.5–4.5 mm	4.5–5.5 mm	5.5–6.5 mm	6.5–9 mm	9 mm and larger
RECOMMENDED HOOK RANGE	B-1 to E-4	E-4 to 7	7 to I-9	I-9 to K-10½	K-10½ to M-13	M-13 and larger

abbreviations

Looking at a knitting pattern for the first time can feel like reading a foreign language. The shortened words are used to prevent laborious repetition, and to make the patterns shorter and easier to follow. Special abbreviations used are mentioned in the stitch glossary at the start of individual patterns. The following abbreviations are common to knitting patterns, and are used throughout the book.

KNITTING NEEDLES SIZES	
USA Size	**Millimeters**
0	2
1	2.25
--	2.5
2	2.75
--	3
3	3.25
4	3.5
5	3.75
6	4
7	4.5
8	5
9	5.5
10	6
10.5	6.5
--	7
--	7.5
11	8
13	9
15	10

CROCHET HOOK SIZES	
USA Size	**Millimeters**
B-1	2.25
C-2	2.75
D-3	3.25
E-4	3.5
F-5	3.75
G-6	4
7	4.5
H-8	5
I-9	5.5
J-10	6
K-10½	6.5
L-11	8
M-/N-13	9
N/P-15	10
P/Q	15
Q	16
S	19

[]	work instructions within brackets as many times as directed
()	work instructions within parentheses in the place directed
★★	repeat instructions following the asterisks as directed
★	repeat instructions followng the asterisk as directed
"	inch(es)
alt	alternate
approx.	approximately
beg	begin/beginning
bet	between
BO	bind off
C2R	cable 2 right
CC	contrasting color
cm	centimetres
cn	cable needle
CO	cast on
cont	continue
dec	decrease
dpn	double-pointed needle(s)
Fl	front loops
foll	follow/follows/following
g	gram
inc	increase
k or K	knit
k2tog	knit two stitches together

kwise	knitwise
LH	left hand
LPC	left purl cross
lp(s)	loop(s)
m	meters
M1	make one—an increase
M1 p-st	make one purl stitch
MC	main color
mm	millimetre(s)
oz	ounce(s)
p or P	purl
pat	pattern
pm	place marker
p2tog	purl 2 stitches together
prev	previous
psso	pass slipped stitch over
pwise	purlwise
rem	remaining
rep	repeat(s)
rev st st	reverse stockinette stitch
RH	right hand
rnd(s)	round(s)
RC	right cross
RPC	right purl cross
RS	right side
sk	skip
sk2p	slip1, knit 2 together, pass slip stitch over
skp	slip, knit, pass stitch over
sl	slip

sl1k	slip 1 knitwise
sl1p	slip 1 purlwise
ss	slip the stitch(es)
ssk	slip, slip, knit 2 stitches together
sssk	slip, slip, slip knit 3 stitches together
st(s)	stitches
St st	stockinette stitch
tbl	through back loop
tog	together
WS	wrong side
w&t	wrap and turn
wyib	with yarn in back
wyif	with yarn in front
yd(s)	yard(s)
yfwd	yarn forward
yo	yarn over
yrn	yarn around needle
yon	yarn over needle

CROCHET ABBREVIATIONS

ch	chain
dc	double crochet
hdc	half double crochet
sc	single crochet
Sl st	slip stitch
tr	treble

Acknowledgments

They say it takes a village to raise a child. It also takes a village to create a book as well. I could never accomplish any of this without the help of my friend and amazing knitter Joyce Nordstrom, and her crew. Thank you for all you many hours of help and for keeping me on track. My creativity is always kept active by my wonderful children Heather and Jonathan, and my grandson Johnny and granddaughter Veronica. A big hug to Tom my husband and the man responsible for making me laugh, especially when I'm on a tight deadline. I also want to thank my friend and one of my creative touchstones, BJ Berti. Thanks for pulling it all together and listening when I'm not sure that a design will really work.

Sources for supplies

Contact the companies listed below for purchasing and mail-order information.

yarn

Berroco
14 Emdale Road, Uxbridge, MA 01569
www.berroco.com

Caron International
PO Box 222, Washington, NC 27889
www.caron.com

Cascade Yarns
1224 Andover Park East, Tukwila, WA 98188
www.cascadeyarns.com

Classic Elite Yarns
122 Western Avenue, Lowell, MA 01851
www.classiceliteyarns.com

Coats & Clark/Red Heart
PO Box 12229, Greenville, SC 29612-0229
www.coatsandclark.com

Lion Brand Yarn
135 Kero Road, Carlstadt, NJ 07072
www.lionbrand.com

Patons
320 Livingstone Avenue South, Listowel,
ON, Canada, N4W 3H3
www.patonsyarns.com

Tahki/Stacy Charles Inc.
70–30 80th St., Building 36, Ridgewood, NY 11385
www.tahkistacycharles.com

Westminster Fibers Inc./Rowan Yarn
4 Townsend West, Unit 8, Nashua, NH 03063
www.knitrowan.com

ribbon

Mokuba New York
55 W.39th St, New York, NY 10019
212 869 8900